THE
VIKING

THE
VIKING

Alan Baker

John Wiley & Sons, Inc.

Published by John Wiley & Sons, Inc., Hoboken, New Jersey
Published simultaneously in Canada

For general information about our other products and services, please contact our
Customer Care Department within the United States at (800) 762-2974, outside the
United States at (317) 572-3993 or fax (317) 572-4002.

Wiley also publishes its books in a variety of electronic formats. Some content that ap-
pears in print may not be available in electronic books. For more information about
Wiley products, visit our web site at www.wiley.com

Library of Congress Cataloging-in-Publication Data:

Baker, Alan.
The Viking / Alan Baker.
p. cm.
ISBN 0-471-43049-8 (Cloth)
1. Vikings. 2. Civilization, Viking. 3. Discoveries in geography—Norse. I. Title.
DL65.B28 2004
948'.022—dc21   2003010750

Printed in the United States of America

10 9 8 7 6 5 4 3 2 1

Contents

I kill without compunction,
And remember all my killings.
— King Harald Hardradi

Introduction
Origins

Things have not gone well now for a long time at home or abroad, but there has been devastation and persecution in every district again and again, and the English have been for a long time now completely defeated and too greatly disheartened through God's anger; and the pirates so strong with God's consent that often in battle one puts to flight ten, and sometimes less, sometimes more, all because of our sins . . . what else is there in all these events except God's anger clear and visible over His people?
— Archbishop Wulfstan of York,
Sermon of the Wolf to the English, A.D. 1014

The Terror from the North

The Vikings are among the fiercest and most feared warriors in history. Their three-hundred-year-long tale is one of violent battle, adventure, and arduous voyages of exploration, including the discovery of North America five centuries before Christopher Columbus. Their reputation as savage and fearsome warriors is certainly well deserved; but there is much more to the Vikings and their history than the brutal warfare, bloody conquest, and merciless pillage for which they became legendary throughout the world. They were not only indomitable fighters but also farmers, sailors, and traders. They were superb craftsmen and fearless explorers; and their mythology and religious beliefs, while redolent with images of battle and glorious death, were as richly conceived and beautiful as those of any other ancient people.

The Viking Age lasted from about A.D. 800 to 1100. For centuries, Europeans had known little of the harsh and strikingly beautiful lands lying to the north, and even less of the tough, self-reliant people inhabiting them. The people of Europe had little reason to wonder what lay beyond their own horizons; such was the peace and prosperity they enjoyed, thanks to strong rulers such as the Frankish emperor Charlemagne and King Offa of Mercia. So confident were people of their safety, which had not been this widespread since the fall of the Roman Empire, that their ports and towns were undefended, as were the monasteries, whose inhabitants trusted unequivocally in the protective power of God.

They were to experience a rude awakening in the form of sudden, vicious, and totally unexpected attacks by terrifying marauders from the North, who plundered and slaughtered without mercy. These savage attackers were pagans, and their total disregard for the sanctity of church property and members made them even more shocking to the people who listened with mounting fear and trepidation to the tales of their barbarity.

The Vikings' ability to strike suddenly and virtually without warning was due to their impressive talents as seamen and shipbuilders. Their vessels were sleek, fast, and exceptionally well built; and whenever their square sails were sighted, the people of western Europe could be certain that death, pillage, and slavery were not far behind. The Viking longships could strike almost anywhere along a coast, and navigable rivers carried them far inland; it was not just coastal communities who trembled at the very thought of these northern marauders.

The first Viking attacks concentrated on monasteries and coastal communities, and the raiders' goals were simple: to acquire as much portable wealth as possible, and to take captives who could either be held for ransom or sold into slavery. However, these did not remain their only objectives, for later the fearsome Norse people turned their attention to long-range exploration, colonization, and trade, activities that would have a lasting effect on the history of western and eastern Europe. In addition, they themselves would ultimately change in profound ways, accepting the teachings of Christianity and abandoning their pagan beliefs.

The Vikings spread outward from their homelands in Norway, Sweden, and Denmark, and the range of their activities was truly impressive. Not only were the effects of their activities felt across the known world, they even extended beyond it as far as the eastern coast of North America. There was not one part of the European coastline that was entirely safe from Viking raids, which extended as far south as the Mediterranean and North Africa. While the Danes and Norwegians moved south and west in their quest for new lands and the riches they contained, the Swedes struck out for the eastern lands, along Russia's mighty rivers and across the Black Sea and the Caspian Sea, eventually to attack that superb yet flawed jewel of European civilization, Constantinople.

The Faeroe Islands, Iceland, and Greenland, those great stepping-stones across the Atlantic Ocean, knew their presence; and tales told by Scandinavian poets and saga writers of their struggles against the fearsome elements in those places are among the most exciting and powerful in world literature. The Vikings' tireless search for valuable items to trade, including furs and walrus ivory, took them far into the icy waters of the Arctic, as far north as Melville Bay in the far north of Greenland.

Although the victims of their raids in the rest of Europe could be forgiven for thinking so, the Vikings did not consider themselves a Scandinavian force standing in unity against the rest of the world. When the opportunities arose, Vikings did not think twice about mounting raids on their own people, and their slaves included other Norse men and women, as well as those from elsewhere on the European continent. Given the brutal nature of their expeditions, it is easy for us to think of all Scandinavians of the period as Vikings — that is, frightful and incredibly violent pagan barbarians with battle-axes eternally raised in preparation to hack the life from anyone who stood in the way of their rapacious plunder. However, this is far from the truth. Most Scandinavians were actually peace-loving farmers, craftsmen, and traders whose minds rarely if ever entertained the notion of violent conquest. When such notions did enter their heads, it was often as a means to an end, a temporary occupation that lasted just long enough to acquire sufficient wealth to buy oneself a piece of land sufficient to support oneself and one's family.

The origin of the word "Viking" is rather obscure. It may be derived from the Old Norse *vikingr,* meaning one who plunders. However, it is open to interpretation. The famous Icelandic historian Magnus Magnusson has this to say in *The Vikings:*

> The word "Viking" is itself a bit of a puzzle. It may be related to the Old Norse word *vík,* meaning "bay" or "creek"; so a "Viking" meant someone who kept his ship in a bay, either for trading or raiding. Others look for a derivation in the Old English word *wic,* borrowed from the Latin *vicus,* meaning a camp or a trading-place; so a "Viking" might mean a warrior or a trader — or both.

To the Scandinavians, the Viking was the epitome of bravery and strength, and young men went on expeditions to prove that they were worthy of respect. The saga writers composed many lines in praise of the Viking warrior, as in this extract from chapter 40 of *Egil's Saga,* probably written by Snorri Sturluson:

My mother once told me
She'd buy me a longship,
A handsome-oared vessel
To go sailing with Vikings:
To stand at the stern-post
And steer a fine warship
Then head back for harbor
And hew down some foemen.

To those whom they attacked and enslaved during the
Viking Age, they represented something slightly different:
they were not only hated and feared plunderers, but also instruments of God's punishment. Archbishop Wulfstan's words
of desperation and lament quoted at the beginning of this introduction were written following the defeat of the English
by the Viking Svein Fork-Beard in 1014. To the medieval
mind, such awful attacks by screaming barbarians could not
but be interpreted as manifestations of God's extreme displeasure with His people. However, there is, of course, far more
to the Viking Age than the wrath of an angry deity.

Without doubt, the principal factor in the Viking expansion was the need for land. Rising populations put greater
and greater pressure on the land available for cultivation, and
as settlements grew in number and size, the demand for tools
resulted in increased iron production. Even before the Viking Age, people were leaving Scandinavia; for instance, the
Goths, Burgundians, and Vandals who invaded the Roman
Empire in the fifth century A.D. believed that their people
had originated in Scandinavia. The population-pressure the-
ory is, however, only partly correct, and can only be applied
to western Norway; there is no evidence to suggest that it
was a problem in the rest of Scandinavia. Indeed, the earliest Scandinavian settlements, in the early ninth century, were
established on the northern and western isles of Scotland and
the Faeroes by Norwegians.

In its initial stages, the Viking expansion was motivated by

the desire for wealth, and the seizure of land overseas by the
fact that the Vikings preferred owning land to renting it from
someone else. It was nearly a hundred years before the
Vikings established any major settlements. Iceland was only
settled in the late ninth century, and it was roughly at this
time that the Danes settled eastern England. By the beginning of the tenth century, Norwegians began to settle in
northwestern England. In addition, we must consider the
importance of advances in shipbuilding techniques during
the eighth century. Rowing boats were fine for short-range
raids but were not suitable for long voyages. The development of the seagoing sailing ship widened the Vikings'
sphere of operations considerably, allowing them to descend
on places much farther afield.

Another key element in Viking expansion was undoubtedly trade, which they initially conducted with the Baltic
lands. The items traded included furs and skins, amber, eider-
down, and whetstones. A major trading center was established
at Ribe, on the western coast of Jutland; other important
centers were at Hedeby in the southeast of Jutland, Birka on
Lake Mälaren in eastern Sweden, and Wolin near the Oder
River estuary. Most of the trade goods had been gathered as
tribute from the Saami, Finns, and Balts who inhabited the
lands producing the best furs. In *The Oxford Illustrated History
of the Vikings,* the editor and historian Peter Sawyer cites a
ninth-century English text that includes some interesting information provided by a Norwegian named Ottar, who was
a guest at the English king Alfred's court. Ottar received
tribute from the Saami:

> That tribute consists of the skins of beasts, the feathers
> of birds, whale-bone, and ship-ropes made from walrus-
> hide and sealskin. Each pays according to his rank. The
> highest in rank has to pay fifteen marten skins, five rein-
> deer skins, one bearskin, and ten measures of feathers,
> and a jacket of bearskin or otterskin, and two ship-ropes.

Each of these must be sixty ells long, one made of walrus hide, the other from seal.

While the Scandinavians were collecting tribute in the form of goods that they then sold in the markets of western Europe, Arab merchants were moving up into Europe from the south, bringing with them their high-quality silver coins, or *dirhems*. The establishment of trading contacts with the Swedes provided them with a new incentive for eastern expansion.

The commercial links between Scandinavia and western Europe encouraged the Vikings to conduct more frequent raids. The frigid waters of the Baltic were the scene of countless pirate attacks by Vikings on merchant ships, and it is possible that during these attacks the Vikings learned of the rich and unguarded settlements and monasteries lying complacently on the coastlines to the south.

The Scandinavians were well known by the Anglo-Saxons and Franks before the raids began in earnest. According to historian John Haywood in *The Penguin Historical Atlas of the Vikings:*

> The circumstances of [an] early Viking raid, on Portland c. 789 . . . suggest that the Anglo-Saxons were already familiar with Scandinavian merchants. Three ships from Hörthaland (in Norway) arrived at the port. The king's reeve Beaduheard, believing them to be merchants, ordered the crews to go to the royal residence at Dorchester: Beaduheard was killed for his trouble. Small-scale pirate raids like this continued to prey on coastal settlements and merchant shipping until the twelfth century.

Another important reason for Viking expansion was the turbulent state of Scandinavian politics. There were many men who, through the possession of royal blood, could lay reasonable claim to kingship, and the resulting disputes over succession were frequently extremely violent affairs. If the loser in these power struggles survived, he was invariably faced with exile from his homeland, and he had little choice but to leave the shores of Scandinavia to seek wealth, power, and prestige in distant lands. If his deeds were sufficiently courageous and profitable, such a man would gather to himself a small army of loyal warriors, with whom he might return home one day to make another bid for domestic power.

The Viking Homelands

The Vikings were incredibly tough, resilient people; these were the qualities required by the starkly beautiful lands in which they lived and worked. The three Scandinavian countries Denmark, Sweden, and Norway occupy an area of land stretching 2,000 kilometers (1,243 miles), from the Jutland Peninsula to the Arctic Circle, or half the length of Europe measured north to south. These three countries only began to develop as well-defined political units during the three centuries of the Viking Age.

Norway boasts the highest mountain in northern Europe — Galdhøpiggen, at 8,100 feet above sea level, and the country's mountainous regions are permanently covered with ice and snow. The gigantic mountain range that dominates the country was called the Keel by the Vikings, and the coast is protected from the icy battering of the Atlantic Ocean by a line of rocks and small islands, the Skerry Guard. The river valleys and the fjords that indent the serrated edge of the Norwegian coast contain strips of agricultural land, while to the south lie fertile plains. In spite of its magnificent harshness, Norway in the Viking Age was home to a wide variety of wild animals, which the Norwegians hunted for their meat and fur. Reindeer and elk, wolves, bears, wolverines, and foxes roamed amid the frigid beauty of the landscape, while the sea churned with fish, seals, whales, and walrus. Food was plentiful, as was the Norwegians' growing desire for trade with and exploration of the lands lying to the south and west.

Like Norway, the highest regions of Sweden, lying immediately to the east, are permanently embraced by ice and snow, and it is from here that the many glittering rivers flow toward the coastal plain and the Gulf of Bothnia. The vast lakes Mälaren, Vänern, and Vättern lie amid fertile lowlands. The national borders were not as they are today, and the southern Swedish provinces of Skåne and Halland were part of Denmark in the Viking Age. Sweden's coastline is shadowed by numerous islands and skerries, the largest of which are Öland and Gotland, in the Baltic. Once again in common with Norway, Sweden possessed huge hunting and fishing resources, as well as vast forests to supply wood, and enormous iron deposits. Sweden enjoyed many trade connections with Denmark, as well as less frequent contacts with the Lapps in the Far North.

Denmark is far smaller than its neighbors to the north. It is fewer than 250 miles long and is very flat. Jutland is the main part of the country, the rest being composed of islands. The milder climate meant that agriculture was the main occupation during the Viking Age, and was of far greater importance than hunting and fishing. The southernmost region of Scandinavia, Denmark naturally enjoyed many more political and cultural contacts with its southern neighbors than Norway and Sweden.

While it is tempting to think of the Vikings as a single cultural and social entity, this was not the case. The vastness of Scandinavia meant that its people and their ways of life varied considerably from place to place. There were variations in the gods they worshiped and in their legal systems. Nevertheless, as the Danish historian Else Roesdahl notes in her book *The Vikings,* Scandinavia itself was "a defined . . . geographical entity in the Viking Age," its vast natural resources making it self-sufficient and its physical location ensuring its remoteness from other European politics and cultures. Roesdahl continues:

The most important inhabited areas were near the coast and communication across great distances was easy in the very efficient ships of the period, while sledges and skis over firm ice and snow made travel inland easy in the winter. Naturally, routes were also found through the large open valleys across the Scandinavian peninsula in the summer. As a result there was a vigorous exchange of goods and ideas over long distances and there is much evidence of political and military contacts, peaceful as well as hostile.

The Early Scandinavians

During the last Ice Age, about thirteen thousand years ago, Scandinavia was home to nomadic hunters who had followed the migrations of reindeer herds across the northern German tundra. When the vast ice sheets began to retreat about eight thousand years ago, hunter-gatherers established a permanent presence, although they still moved around a great deal, exploiting the seasonal animals and plants. The Vikings probably were direct descendants of these first hardy human settlers, who adopted agriculture in about 4000 B.C., and replaced their flint tools with bronze ones about two thousand years later.

Although these Neolithic farmers were separated from each other, the large megalithic communal tombs they left behind strongly imply that they felt a common identity with each other. The first villages appeared during the Bronze Age. The presence of a single large building surrounded by smaller buildings implies that these communities were ruled by chieftains, and this is further borne out by the presence of richly furnished graves.

Following an initial decline at the beginning of the Early Iron Age (500 B.C.–A.D. 1), the Scandinavian population underwent a steady increase lasting for the remainder of the Iron Age. According to John Haywood in *The Penguin Historical Atlas of the Vikings*:

It was in the Roman Iron Age (A.D. 1–400) and the succeeding Germanic Iron Age (400–800) that Scandinavian society developed its familiar Viking characteristics.

Because of the virtual absence of literary sources, it is impossible to reconstruct the political and social changes of the period in any detail, but they can be drawn in outline on the basis of archaeological evidence and by comparison with the better-documented Germanic peoples to the south.

The presence in Scandinavia of Roman weapons in votive deposits suggests that the Norse peoples were in conflict with Germanic tribes to the south, who in turn were in contact with the Roman Empire. At this time, Scandinavia began to be dominated by an elite class of warriors, and the luxury goods found in their graves (such as glass and jewelry) imply that Scandinavia was linked with Rome either by direct or indirect trade.

The Germanic tribes were considerably enriched by their contact with Rome: they were paid handsomely for both their goods and their military service. To the Scandinavians, who were far worse off, they must have presented an enticing target for plunder. It is a reasonable supposition that the individual who mounted successful raids would be admired and respected more than his fellows, and the combination of wealth and battle prowess would result in a rise in status to that of chieftain or even king.

Religion

Scandinavian theology, while incredibly vibrant (not to mention bloody), was not based on concepts of universal good and evil, nor were its ideas on the afterlife particularly clearly defined. The religion of the early Scandinavians, and of the Vikings themselves prior to the conversion to Christianity in A.D. 1000, was pagan, and as such was far more concerned with the observance of rituals (including sacrifices of animals and sometimes humans) than the cultivation of one's personal spirituality.

The Scandinavians' visualization of the universe is both fascinating and intricate. They believed that it consisted of three disclike planes separated from each other by empty space. The uppermost level was called Asgard, the home of the race of Norse gods known as the Aesir. They were proud, capricious, and violent, with a love of battle and slaughter, and lived with their goddess wives in a colossal citadel that they had conned a giant into building for them. This also was the location of Valhalla, the Hall of the Slain, where dead warriors would fight all day and drink and feast all night, their battle wounds miraculously healed.

On this highest realm lived another race of gods, the Vanir, whose home was called Vanaheim. They were fertility gods, and much more disposed toward peace than the Aesir, although they could be provoked to violence on occasion.

The second level was called Midgard, the middle world and the domain of human beings. Midgard was surrounded by an incredibly vast circular ocean inhabited by Jormungand, the gigantic world serpent who completely encircled the world of men and whose thrashing coils caused sea storms. Humans shared the world of Midgard with the giants, who lived in Jotunheim, far to the east beyond a mountain range; and with the dwarfs, who lived underground in Nidavellir. The dark elves also lived close by, in the land of Svartalfheim (although it seems that they were very similar, if not identical, to the dwarfs).

The realms of Asgard and Midgard were connected by a rainbow bridge called Bifrost (Quivering Roadway). The great Icelandic saga writer Snorri Sturluson wrote of Bifrost in *The Prose Edda*:

> You will have seen it, but maybe you call it the rainbow. It has three colors and is very strong, and made with more skill and cunning than other structures. . . . The red you see in the rainbow is flaming fire. If it were possible for all who wanted to go over Bifrost to do so, the frost ogres and cliff giants would scale heaven. There are

many beautiful places in heaven, and they are all under divine protection.

In his book *The Norse Myths,* the poet and folklorist Kevin Crossley-Holland points out the impossibility of precisely defining the physical relationship of the different realms in the Norse universe:

> [I]n a number of myths . . . gods and giants made an overland journey direct from Asgard to Jotunheim without passing through Midgard. How can they have done so? It would seem physically impossible unless we tilt the Asgard- and Midgard-levels so that, at one point, they actually touch each other! This kind of problem demonstrates the limitations of logic in trying to define precisely where the worlds stood in relation to one another. It is best simply to bear in mind that the structure of the universe was basically tricentric and assume that the Norsemen themselves were rather vague and unconcerned about more exact geography.

The third and final level in the Norse universe was Niflheim, the world of the dead. It was a dreadful place, dark and cold, and ruled by a terrifying goddess named Hel, who lived in a citadel of the same name. It was here that evil men came to die a second time.

The three levels of the universe were connected by the great ash tree Yggdrasil, which almost certainly means "Odin's horse." Yggdrasil has three roots — one anchored in Asgard, one in Jotunheim, and the third in Niflheim. The eternal tree nourishes various beasts that gnaw at its roots and leaves. A dragon called Nidhogg chews at the roots, while deer and goats eat the new shoots sprouting from its branches. Meanwhile, a squirrel runs up and down the trunk, carrying insults from Nidhogg to an eagle perched in the uppermost branches.

Yggdrasil is an example of what mythologists call the World

Tree, a feature common to many belief systems throughout the world. As Crossley-Holland notes, such images are to be found in the Vedic literature of India and Chinese mythology.

Migration

The great voyages of discovery that would culminate in the astonishing achievement of the finding of North America began with the Norse settlement of the Faeroes, a remote and mountainous collection of islands jutting out of the savage North Sea northwest of Shetland. The *Faereyinga Saga* states that the first Viking settler was named Grímur Kamban. Those who followed him came from the western coast of Norway. It seems that settlement began in about 825, since this is when an Irish monk named Dicuil complained that his brethren had been frightened away by Norsemen. (Christian monks would often wander through the northern latitudes in search of isolated places where they might devote themselves to God.)

Although it is impossible to grow crops on the Faeroes, the islands will support sheep and cattle, and this formed the basis of the economy for the first settlers. Little is known of the early history of Viking settlement on these inhospitable, windswept lumps of rock. All we know is that they seem to have been claimed by a group of aristocratic families. In the last decade of the ninth century, the islands were brought under the control of the kings of Norway.

When Gardar the Swede was blown off course while voyaging to the Hebrides in about 860, he made landfall near the Eastern Horn of Iceland. He spent the next year circumnavigating the island and, deciding that he liked the look of the land, opted to set up home there. Not long afterward, another explorer, Floki Vilgerdarson, decided to settle permanently on the island. He took with him livestock and three ravens dedicated to Odin, and dropped anchor at Bardaströnd, on the western coast. According to the *Landnámabók* (Book of Settlements), written in the twelfth century:

The fjord teemed with fish of all kinds, and [Floki and his companions] were so busy fishing that they paid no heed to gathering hay for the winter; and that winter, all their livestock died. The following spring was an extremely cold one. Floki climbed a high mountain and looked north towards the coast, and saw a fjord choked with drift-ice; and so they called the country *Ísland* [Iceland], and that has been its name ever since.

Floki was less than impressed with this new land, and returned home to Norway as soon as he could, without a good word to say of the place. However, two of his companions, Herjólf and Thórólf, decided to make a go of it, and presently were joined by other settlers. In those days the climate was warmer than it is today, by about 1 degree Centigrade, which meant that fully a quarter of the land was tree-covered, whereas today the figure is closer to 1 percent.

Soon more and more settlers voyaged to Iceland, mainly because they could not tolerate the growing power of the Norwegian king Harald Fine-Hair, who was ruling the local chieftains with an iron fist. The Norsemen did not take kindly to being told what to do by anyone, not even the king, and so many sold their lands and left the country, taking their families, friends, slaves, and livestock with them.

The Norwegians were soon joined by Swedes, Danes, and Scandinavians from the Hebrides, and by the mid-tenth century nearly all the good grazing land had been claimed. A group of men called the *goðar* assumed leadership of the colony, and it was their task to settle disputes at the district assemblies (known as *things*) and protect the interests of smaller and less powerful landowners. The islandwide assembly, the Althing, was set up to establish common laws. The island was divided into four quarters whose chieftains (and only they) could vote in the Althing.

Iceland was converted to Christianity in 1000, and the first bishopric was established at Skalholt in 1056. Iceland enjoyed a stable government until the thirteenth century, when civil war broke out as a result of power struggles between chiefly families. The civil war resulted in Iceland coming under direct rule from Norway in 1263.

In this book we will look at the history of the Vikings, their culture and society. Chapter 1, "Warriors of the North," will describe how the Norsemen descended into western Europe, mounting vicious, lightning-fast raids on the unguarded shores of the British Isles, France, and the Mediterranean. We also will examine their weapons, battle tactics, and the graceful ships that made their exploits so fantastically successful.

In chapter 2, "Gods and Monsters," we shall return to the fascinating world of Viking mythology and meet the inhabitants of Asgard, the home of the gods, as well as the many other strange beings with whom they occasionally fought, culminating in Ragnarok, the doom of the gods, which sees the destruction and rebirth of the entire universe.

Chapter 3, "Society and Culture," will be devoted to the Norse people at home in Scandinavia, how they lived from day to day, the clothes and jewelry they wore, and the food they cultivated and ate. In this chapter we shall see that there was more to Viking life than bloody warfare and plunder.

In Chapter 4, "Journeys to a New World," we shall follow the Viking explorers across the Atlantic Ocean to the mysterious new world of Vinland in what is now America, drawing on the sagas of the great Snorri Sturluson.

Chapter 5, "New Lives in the East," will examine the migration of the Swedish Vikings into Russia, where they founded a great trading empire that stretched as far as Constantinople, the capital of the Byzantine Empire.

Finally, we shall look at the end of the Viking Age and the legacy left by these fearsome warriors.

1

Warriors of the North

You wiped blood from your greedy
Sword when battle was over.
You fed the ravens with corpses
While wolves howled in the mountains.
The next year, king of warriors,
You spent east in Russia;
Nowhere have I ever heard
Of a greater soldier than you.
> — Bolverk Arnorsson, court poet to
> King Harald Hardradi of Norway

The Vikings in the British Isles

It is a curious quirk of history that the first major Viking raid also became the most famous — or infamous, depending on one's point of view. Following the raid by three Norwegian ships on Portland, at which the reeve Beaduheard was killed (see the introduction), and the construction of coastal defenses by the Mercian king Offa, the Vikings descended in 793 on the famous monastery of St. Cuthbert on the holy island of Lindisfarne, just off the northeastern coast of England. This is how *The Anglo-Saxon Chronicle,* edited and translated by Michael Swanton, described the horrific event:

> 793. In this year terrible portents appeared over North-umbria which sorely affrighted the inhabitants: there were exceptional flashes of lightning, and fiery dragons were seen flying through the air. A great famine followed hard upon these signs; and a little later in that same year, on the 8th of June, the harrying of the heathen miserably destroyed God's church on Lindisfarne by rapine and slaughter.

Tiny, windswept, and completely defenseless, Lindisfarne was home to a group of peaceful monks and was revered as a cradle of Christianity. The day of the raid began like any other, with the monks going about their usual devotional business. But death and disaster were bearing down on them even then. Over the edge of the cold, gray eastern horizon appeared the square sail of a Viking longship. Its snarling dragon-headed prow cut like an ax blade through the waves as it approached the island. With a tortured scrape, keel met sand, and the great vessel came to a halt, disgorging the warriors whom Christians would later come to call "the revenge of Satan."

"And they came to the church of Lindisfarne," writes the chronicler Simeon of Durham in his *Historia Regum* and quoted in Magnusson, "laid everything waste with grievous plundering, trampled the holy places with polluted feet, dug up the altars and seized all the treasures of the holy church." They slaughtered many of the monks, driving them naked out of the monastery and drowning them in the sea; the rest they dragged away into slavery. Simeon, however, was not entirely correct when he wrote that the Vikings took all of the church's treasures: it seems that the monks had at least some warning (the appearance of the ominous sail upon the horizon may well have alerted them to coming danger), and managed to hide some valuables, including the Lindisfarne Gospels.

The attack on Lindisfarne caused the utmost horror and consternation in the Christian Church. In this more secular age, it is difficult to grasp just what a shocking atrocity it was to contemporary Christians. It was seen as an attack on civilization itself, a monstrous assault committed by savage and godless pagans.

When news of the attack reached him at the court of Charlemagne, the Northumbrian scholar Alcuin wrote to Aethelred, king of Northumbria (quoted in Magnusson):

> Lo, it is nearly 350 years that we and our fathers have inhabited this most lovely land, and never before has such terror appeared in Britain as we have now suffered from a pagan race, nor was it thought that such an inroad from the sea could be made. Behold, the church of St Cuthbert spattered with the blood of the priests of God, despoiled of all its ornaments, a place more venerable than all in Britain is given as a prey to pagan peoples.

Like his fellow Christians, Alcuin could not understand why God had allowed this monstrous event to take place. The only possible explanation was that God was punishing His people for being unworthy:

> the calamity of your tribulation saddens me greatly every day, though I am absent; when the pagans desecrated the sanctuaries of God, and poured out the blood of saints around the altar, laid waste the house of our hope, trampled on the bodies of saints in the temple of God, like dung in the street. . . . What assurance is there for the churches of Britain, if St Cuthbert, with so great a number of saints, defends not its own? Either this is the beginning of greater tribulation, or else the sins of the inhabitants have called it upon them. Truly it has not happened by chance, but is a sign that it was well merited by someone. But now, you who are left, stand manfully, fight bravely, defend the camp of God.

Later events were to prove Alcuin correct in his specula-
tion that this was the "beginning of greater tribulation." The
attack on Lindisfarne was merely the first of a string of raids
in which small fleets of about ten or twelve ships launched
swift assaults on coastal areas. These smash-and-grab raids
were extremely difficult to counter, for no one knew when
and where the next would happen, and by the time defensive
forces were gathered and deployed, the Vikings were already
long gone.

These lightning-fast assaults constituted the first phase of
Viking activity; the second phase began after the mid-ninth
century, when the Norsemen built camps so they could
spend the winter in western Europe, closer to their targets.
They established permanent settlements in Scotland and
Ireland, and also concentrated their attentions on Frankia,
which they ruled intermittently until the 880s.

The attacks continued during the third phase, during which
Viking settlements grew in number. In 865 a large Viking
army invaded East Anglia, Northumbria, and Mercia, and
promptly established settlements in those conquered kingdoms. When Alfred the Great repelled their invasion of
Wessex, many Vikings returned to Frankia, but there, too,
they found stout resistance from the Franks, so they returned
to England. However, in the meantime Alfred the Great had
completely reorganized his kingdom's defenses, and the returning Vikings found themselves constantly harassed by the
English until the Vikings finally abandoned Wessex in 896.

England was especially vulnerable to the Vikings' attentions: not only was it composed of fragmented and uncoop-
erative kingdoms, it also possessed an excellent road network,
courtesy of the long-departed Romans, which allowed hostile forces to move quickly and easily across the land. In 865
the Great Army of Danes arrived in East Anglia, with the intention of conquering the country. The Danes were bought
off with a supply of good horses, and made for Northumbria
and the city of York, which they took with ease. The city be-

came the center of a Viking kingdom ruled by puppet kings until 954, when the English king Eadred took control of Northumbria.

The region of the Northeast under the control of the Danes is known as the Danelaw. The victorious English kings allowed the Scandinavians to decide their own laws. The regions comprising the Danelaw were Northumbria, East Anglia, the Five Boroughs of Stamford, Leicester, Derby, Nottingham, Lincoln, and the southeast Midlands. Its southern border was established by a treaty between King Alfred and Guthrum of East Anglia. The effect of this treaty was to divide England into three principal regions: Wessex, English Mercia, and the Danelaw. Although the Danelaw's political independence was relatively short-lived (fifty years at most), its Scandinavian identity was recognized by Alfred and his successors, and also by Knut in the eleventh century and by the Norman conquerors after 1066.

According to the editor and historian Peter Sawyer in *The Oxford Illustrated History of the Vikings:*

> The Danelaw (its name had no currency before the time of Knut) was, we suspect, at no time fully homogeneous, but internal variations in respect of race, density of Norse settlement, political allegiance and social organization, counted for less than its separateness from English England. The evidence of personal coins and moneyers is indicative, and that of language, vocabulary, and place names compulsive, that there was a rapid and heavy settlement of parts of the Danelaw by Scandinavians representing little less than a migration, and recent attempts to minimize the Norse element have been unconvincing.

In 795 the Vikings mounted a raid on a church on Lambey Island near Dublin, Ireland. For the next thirty years or so, the raids proceeded much as they did in England, with swift attacks on undefended coastal settlements, especially churches and monasteries. In the mid-ninth century the attacks became more elaborate and better coordinated, with large fleets of longships sailing up navigable rivers, such as the Shannon, and thus penetrating deep into the Irish hinterland.

The Irish were unable to mount a coordinated defense of their land, mainly because there was so much fighting and strife among the subkings in the five Irish high kingdoms, Ulster, Connacht, Meath, Leinster, and Munster. By 840, Norwegian Vikings had built many fortified camps, the most important of which was at Dublin, and had become a permanent presence. The establishment of permanent settlements had a serious downside, however, for the Vikings living there were now themselves vulnerable to Irish counterattacks. By 847 the Irish resistance had become so effective that many Vikings decided that staying in Ireland had become untenable, and moved to Frankia.

In 851, Danish Vikings took control of Dublin, but were expelled two years later by the Norwegian Olaf the White, who made himself king of Dublin. When his successor Ivar died in 873, the kingdom became politically unstable, and many Vikings left Ireland to concentrate on plundering England and Frankia. Thus began the "Forty Years' Rest," during which Ireland saw very little Viking activity.

The period of rest ended in 914, when the Vikings returned from England and Frankia with renewed vigor, reestablishing themselves in Dublin, from which they had been expelled in 902, and elsewhere on the island. This time the Vikings seemed content to return to their original strategy of penetrating the hinterland along the navigable rivers and conducting swift raids.

The Irish Vikings were driven out of York, which they had seized in 919, by King Athelstan. Olaf Guthfrithsson, king of Dublin, attempted to retake the city in 937, but was defeated by Athelstan at Brunanburh (the exact location of which is unknown) near the Humber estuary. However, in 939 Olaf conquered Northumbria and the Five Boroughs of the Danelaw; but in 944, the English reclaimed York. An exiled king of Norway named Eirik Bloodax, a man with a fearsome reputation for violence, as his name suggests, took York yet again for the Vikings in 948. He was driven out by the Northumbrians, who killed him in 954.

The Viking Age in Ireland finally ended in 1014, with their defeat at the Battle of Clontarf outside Dublin on Good Friday. The victor was Brian Boru, an Irish king who had entertained ambitions of becoming the high king of Ireland but who was killed at the moment of his triumph. The power of the Vikings declined further following their defeat, mainly due to the constant pressure brought to bear on them by the kings of Munster in the south and Meath in the east.

By the year 1000, the Norsemen were converting to Christianity and thus losing much of their Viking identity. They also intermarried with the Irish and began to speak Gaelic. Eventually they came to be known as "Ostmen" (men of the East) rather than Scandinavians.

In Scotland, as in England and Ireland, the earliest attack by the Vikings was on a monastery. The monastery of Colmcille on Iona fell in 795, and for the next fifty years, churches and settlements around the western coasts were mercilessly raided and plundered. Once again, raiding eventually gave way to settling, and by 900 many islands and coastal areas had been settled by Norwegians. While the native Celts in Orkney and Shetland were absorbed by the Viking settlers, the opposite was the case in the Hebrides, where Celts and Norse intermarried.

According to the thirteenth-century *Orkneyinga Saga*, the Norwegian king Harald Fine-Hair sailed to the Northern Isles to annex them for the Norwegian crown:

One summer King Harald Fine-Hair sailed west on a punitive expedition against the Vikings who were raiding the coasts of Norway from their winter-bases in Shetland or the Orkneys; for he had grown tired of their depredations. He subdued Shetland and the Orkneys and the Hebrides, and sailed all the way down to the Isle of Man and destroyed all the settlements there. He fought many battles there, and extended his dominion further west than any king of Norway has done since then.

One of those killed in battle was Ívar, the son of Earl Rögnvald of Møre; so when King Harald set sail for Norway, he gave Earl Rögnvald the Orkneys and Shetland as compensation for his son. Earl Rögnvald in turn transferred both countries to his brother Sigurð, who was King Harald's prow-man. When the king sailed back to Norway he bestowed on Sigurð the title of Earl, and Sigurð stayed behind on the islands.

The Viking presence in Scotland served to profoundly influence the existing power structure, which had been defined by struggles among four ethnic groups: the Highland Picts, the Scots of Dalriada, the Britons of Strathclyde, and the Anglo-Saxons of Northumbria. All of these groups suffered at the hands of the Vikings; however, the Scots emerged as the strongest group, and conquered the others between 844 and 973, ultimately creating the kingdom of Scotland.

Frankia

Like a relentless rain of terror and death, the Vikings plunged farther south, attacking the monasteries and vulnerable settlements in the coastal regions in the northwestern portion of the Frankish Empire. It was vitally important to prevent the Norse raiders from sailing up the rivers and penetrating deep into the country, so the Frankish emperor Charlemagne deployed fleets on the inland waterways to defend the hinterland.

However, there was at least one occasion, in 810, when a

Viking raid was mounted as much to display strength as merely to plunder. The Danish king Godfred, mindful of Frankish expansion on his southern border, attacked the empire's Frisian coast before the Frankish forces had time to mount a defense. When Charlemagne died in 815, his successor, Louis the Pious, concentrated on maintaining coastal defenses; but by the 830s internal conflicts within the empire had resulted in a weakening of those defenses, and within ten years the Vikings had managed to penetrate the Rhine River on four occasions to attack the empire's richest port, Dorestad.

The internal conflicts raging within the Frankish Empire continued after the death of Louis the Pious, whose three sons — Lothar, Charles the Bald, and Louis the German — squabbled over their inheritance. This did not escape the attention of the Vikings, who took the opportunity to intensify their raids and establish permanent camps from which they could attack Frankish towns and monasteries throughout the year. The kingdom of Charles the Bald occupied much of modern-day France, the eastern border extending from Antwerp (in today's Belgium), to the north, to the mouth of the Rhone River on the Mediterranean coast. It bordered Lothar's kingdom to the east and occupied the Netherlands, part of Germany and northern Italy. Louis the German's kingdom included Germany, Czechoslovakia, and Austria to the east.

Of the three Frankish kingdoms, Charles the Bald's fared worst from the Vikings, due to a combination of its long coastline, profusion of navigable rivers, and the internal problems from which he was suffering. In 843 a rebel count joined forces with the Vikings to seize Nantes, near the Atlantic coast, and in 858 Charles was forced to abandon his siege of the Viking camp on the island of Oissel in the Seine river when Louis the German marched into his kingdom. Charles had no option but to pay the Vikings to stop raiding his kingdom; and although this ultimately had the effect of encouraging them to increase their raids, it placated them in the short term, giving Charles the time he needed to deal with his internal enemies.

Lothar's kingdom also suffered considerably from the Vikings' attentions, but he managed to solve the problem by playing the Norsemen off against each other, offering lands in Frisia and the Rhine estuary to some Viking chiefs on the condition that they repel the raids of other Vikings. Of the three kings, Louis the German had the least trouble from the Vikings, mainly due to the very short coastline in the north of his kingdom, which made it a much less attractive target compared to his brothers' lands.

In the year 845, a Danish Viking named Ragnar took 120 ships into the Seine. In response, Charles the Bald deployed his army on the banks of the river. This was a mistake: Ragnar simply attacked and defeated the smaller force, and hanged 111 prisoners while their comrades in the larger force watched helplessly. This completely destroyed Frankish morale, and Ragnar was able to reach his objective, Paris, which he sacked on Easter Sunday. He was only persuaded to leave by Charles the Bald's offer of 7,000 pounds of silver. This was the first time the Vikings were paid protection money (known in England as danegeld). It would not be the last.

In 847, all three kings went to see King Horik of Denmark, and threatened war if he did not bring the raiders under control. He refused. In the 860s, a monk named Ermentarius of Noirmoutier described the awful depredations of the Vikings in his *History of the Miracles and Translations of Saint Philibert:*

The number of ships grows: the endless stream of Vikings never ceases to increase. Everywhere the Christians are victims of massacres, burnings, plunderings: the Vikings conquer all in their path, and no one resists them: they seize Bordeaux, Périgeux, Limoges, Angoulême and Toulouse. Angers, Tours and Orléans are annihilated and an innumerable fleet sails up the Seine and the evil grows in the whole region. Rouen is laid waste, plundered and burned: Paris, Beauvais and Meaux taken, Melun's strong fortress levelled to the ground, Chartres occupied, Evreux and Bayeux plundered, and every town besieged.

Everyone suffered to some degree, even those outside the towns, churches, and monasteries, for the Vikings were paid numerous ransoms, which were raised by imposing taxes on everyone, even the poor. The Vikings also plundered small settlements and took many slaves from the rural population.

Having dealt with the political strife within his kingdom, Charles the Bald embarked on the task of dealing with the Viking threat. He built new fortifications and repaired the town walls originally built by the Romans. Across the Seine and Loire Rivers he built sturdy, fortified bridges to protect Paris and the lands at the heart of his kingdom. While Paris was well protected, the lands and towns to the north and west were left vulnerable to Viking attacks. The fortified bridges, such as the one at Pont de l'Arche on the Seine near Pitres, were protected by garrisons in large wood and stone forts on each bank of the river. Pont de l'Arche was completed in about 870, and deterred the Vikings for the next ten years. However, the bridge and its forts were finally destroyed by Vikings in 885.

His army's performance was uneven, to say the least: in 866 they met the Vikings at Melun on the Seine, just south of Paris, and fled in disarray. Charles was forced to pay the Norsemen 4,000 pounds of silver to leave the area. Seven years later, however, the Frankish army laid siege to the Viking camp at Angers in the west of the country and succeeded in driving them out.

Charles's tactic of setting the Vikings against each other was likewise rather hit and miss. On one occasion in 860, he bribed the Viking chief Weland to mount an attack from his base on the Somme against the Vikings occupying Oissel on the Seine. He agreed, but the Seine Vikings simply offered him a bigger bribe of 6,000 pounds of silver to let them escape,

and then returned the following year to continue their plundering. Eventually, in 866, Charles managed to get rid of the
Seine Vikings by paying them to leave.

In the 860s the Frankish regional counts began to mount
significant defenses against the Norse invaders, more so even
than the king. In 862, Count Robert of Angers captured no
fewer than twelve Viking warships and killed their crews. His
success lay in the fact that he could mobilize his own forces
to deal with local trouble far more quickly and effectively
than the king, with his centralized forces. Although this locally organized resistance played an important part in the decline of Viking influence in the late ninth century, it was the
successful invasion of England by the Danish Great Army
that persuaded the Norsemen to leave Frankia.

This leavetaking was only temporary, however: Following
Alfred the Great's successful defense of his Kingdom of
Wessex, Viking forces landed at Calais in 879. Acquiring
horses, they ravaged northern Flanders and made for Ghent,
where they joined a Viking winter camp. This was the beginning of a highly successful raiding tactic that would be used
for more than a decade: every year, the Vikings left their
camp behind and moved on to a new one, frequently a
monastery on a navigable river, from which they would sally
forth and plunder the surrounding area. When they had
sucked Flanders and the Rhineland dry, they sailed up the
Seine toward Paris, only to find their way blocked by two
fortified bridges. Their demands to be let through were ignored, and so they tried to attack and destroy the bridges.
The Parisians held their bridges for a year, until they were finally relieved by Emperor Charles the Fat (son of Louis the
German). After listening to their demands, Charles the Fat
decided to allow them through so they could sail past Paris
and continue their raiding along the Seine and the Marne.
He even gave them provisions and 700 pounds of silver as
added incentives. This apparently humiliating climb-down
by Charles led ultimately to his deposition in 888. But
Charles had a reason for letting the Vikings pass instead of

fighting them: he encouraged the Norsemen to spend the winter in Burgundy, where he was having serious trouble with his own subjects. Magnus Magnusson writes in *The Vikings:*

> There is no mistaking the policy: for a large enough price the Vikings could not only be bought off, but used. They had become an undeniable factor in the political scene in Frankia. Viking war-bands, weary perhaps of the long years at the oar and sated with pillage, could now be induced to settle in the lands they had ravaged, there to form a new kind of bulwark against further attack. Viking dynasties would be formed on Frankish soil, flourish for a time, and then die out or be taken over.

Following the deposition of Charles the Fat, Charlemagne's empire was shared out, and the new king of Neustria, the western kingdom, was Count Odo, who had fought bravely to defend Paris prior to Charles's capitulation. Odo possessed far more fighting spirit, and with a combination of military force and bribery, he drove the Vikings from the Seine in 889.

After an unsuccessful invasion attempt in Brittany, the Vikings turned toward the East Frankish kingdom, where King Arnulf also fought bravely against them, allowing them no rest and harrying them to such an extent that they found it impossible to establish permanent camps there.

By 892, most of the Vikings on the Seine had left to concentrate on raiding targets in England, and those who remained decided to take a break from the warrior's life and settle down. Their leader was named Hrólf, and he was so huge that no horse could carry his weight and he had to go everywhere on foot. He was therefore known as Göngu-Hrólf, or Hrólf the Ganger. He is better known in history as Rollo, the founder of the duchy of Normandy.

Rollo's activities in France are unknown before 911, when he led a force that besieged Chartres. The Vikings were successfully repelled, however, and King Charles III, deciding to try to make a lasting peace with the Norsemen, summoned Rollo to a meeting. Charles agreed to grant to the Vikings the lands they already occupied. This demonstrated sound, good sense, since the Vikings as settlers would doubtless defend those lands against future Viking invasion. Rollo agreed, and he and his men swore oaths of allegiance to the king. There is an amusing legend regarding Rollo's paying homage to the king. He was supposed to do so by bending down and kissing Charles's foot. Instead, he bent down, grabbed the royal foot, and then stood up to his full height, taking the foot with him and pitching Charles onto his back. Needless to say, the assembled Vikings thought this hilarious, although it is doubtful whether Charles saw the funny side. The agreement resulted in the birth of the Duchy of Normandy, the province of the Northmen. Rollo and his people agreed to convert to Christianity, and Rollo apparently did so enthusiastically.

The arrangement worked extremely well, and the Seine River valley never again suffered from Viking assaults. Rollo, now count of Rouen, was granted further lands around Bayeux, and his successor, William Longsword, acquired the Cotentin Peninsula in 933. Although the region was named after the Northmen, they were very much a minority there, and their long-term influence was slight. Rollo was well aware of the differences between Viking and Frankish concepts of kingship. According to Magnusson: "Whereas the Vikings had favoured a loosely democratic or oligarchic system in which the authority of the king rested upon the freely given support of his subjects, the Franks imposed authority from above." This was the feudal system, in which the king owned all the land and was the ultimate legal authority. Rollo grasped the feudal system and put it into effect, subduing internal rivals and external encroachments. The Duchy of Normandy steadily increased in strength, mounting the successful Conquest of England under Duke William in 1066. Long before that time, however, the duchy had become completely French in its culture, language, and administration.

The Normans successfully blocked the movements of the Vikings along the Seine, so the Norse raiders turned their attention to Brittany, which had hitherto escaped the worst of the raids. In fact, the Vikings were occasionally more useful than dangerous to the Bretons, who expanded their lands to the south and west while the Frankish emperors were distracted by internal strife and Norse raids.

By the early tenth century, Brittany became vulnerable to the Viking threat: the Danes were having serious problems maintaining a foothold in England, and the Vikings were finding it impossible to operate on the Seine. Brittany was there for the taking (as was Ireland), and the raids greatly intensified from 912 onward. The coastal monasteries were the first to fall, abandoned by the terrified monks. Brittany's defenses fell apart in 919, and the nobility promptly fled to Frankia and England, leaving the country wide open to Viking invasion. The Norsemen took Nantes and made it their capital, although they used it only as a military base from which to launch attacks on Frankia. This prompted the Bretons to rebel, but the rebellion was put down. Nevertheless, it had the effect of encouraging an exiled noble, Alan Barbetorte, to invade Brittany in 936. Nantes was retaken the following year, and the Vikings were finally expelled in 939.

The Mediterranean

It is a tribute to their seamanship as well as their daring that Viking ships and fleets made it as far as the western (and possibly the eastern) Mediterranean in about the mid-ninth century. Contact between the Vikings and the Moors of Spain came about as a result of an attempted raid by a fleet of 150 ships on the Spanish Christian Kingdom of Galicia and Asturias in 844.

The Spanish in this northern kingdom of the Iberian Peninsula offered stout resistance to the Norse marauders, and the sea itself battered their mighty ships without mercy.

As a result, the Viking fleet was depleted but still intact when it left the Bay of Biscay and rounded Cape Finisterre, heading south toward Lisbon. For the next two weeks the fleet made a considerable nuisance of itself to shipping in the area before descending on Lisbon and sacking the city in August 844.

The Vikings then headed south once again, along the Atlantic coast of the Moorish Umayyad Emirate of Cordoba, entered the Guadalquivir River, and captured the city of Seville. It was an incredibly bold and audacious assault, for the Viking fleet constituted a comparatively tiny force that penetrated deep into Moorish territory. The Norsemen were well rewarded for their daring: except for the citadel, Seville fell into their hands for a week, and during this brief period they visited untold horrors on the population. The men of the city fell to the Vikings' swords, while their women and children were carried off to the Vikings' base that had been established on the island of Qubtil (Isla Menor) near the mouth of the Guadalquivir.

From Qubtil they mounted raids on the surrounding countryside for the next six weeks, gaining much treasure and many captives. Their success was not to last, however: the Moors of Spain were not so ready to bribe the Vikings to leave them alone as the Franks had been. Once the Moors, under their leader Abd al-Rahman II, had recovered from their initial surprise, they began to coordinate attacks on the Norse invaders by land and water. When a raiding party left the headquarters on Qubtil, Moorish forces would attempt to cut it off, and frequently succeeded. So successful was the Moorish defense of their territory that the gallows in Seville could not handle the number of captured Vikings who were executed, so they were hung from the city's palm trees. The Moors claimed to have captured and killed fourteen hundred men and destroyed thirty ships. The audacious invaders were now in serious trouble, and realized that their only chance of escape lay in their captives, whom the Moors wished to ransom. The Norsemen gladly agreed; so desperate was their situation that they asked that the ransom be paid in food and clothing instead of gold. This particular expedition to the Mediterranean was rather less than successful, and the survivors lost no time in heading north, to comparative safety.

It seems that some civilized discourse existed between the Vikings and Moors, for in the following year, 845, Abd al-Rahman II sent his emissary Al-Ghazal to a Norse king, bearing many gifts for him and his wife. It is uncertain who this king was, but he may have been Horik in Denmark or Turgeis in Ireland. According to the highly respected historian of the Vikings Gwyn Jones in *A History of the Vikings:*

> The northern king, whoever he was, dwelt on a big island in the ocean, gracious with gardens and flowing waters. Near by were other islands inhabited by Majus [the Moorish name for Norsemen], and three days' journey away was the mainland or continent, and here, too, the king held power. The king's wife was named Nod, or Noud, and the gallant, graceful, and 50-year-old Al-Ghazal was delighted to find his wish for a beautiful friendship received in the same amiable spirit as it was offered. And how gratefully there must have fallen on an ear grown wary for an inrushing husband's unreason Noud's assurance that the Majus were too enlightened for jealousy and that northern ladies were free to leave their consorts at will. If the embassy had political or economic consequences, we are not informed of them, but it seems safe to assume that its main purpose was to encourage trade, more particularly in furs and slaves.

The first Viking expedition to the Mediterranean in the 840s was bold and daring enough; but it was the four-year-long expedition of two Vikings, Björn Ironside and Hastein, that would become legendary. It began in 857 in Paris. Abbo of St. Germain de Près writes (quoted in Magnusson):

> Paris! There you sit in the middle of the Seine, in the midst of the rich lands of the Franks, calling out: "I am

a city above all others, sparkling like a queen above them all!" All know you by the splendour of your bearing. Whoever lusts after the wealth of France is paying you homage. An island rejoices to support you, a river embraces you, its arms caressing your walls. Bridges stand on the riverbanks to left and right, towers keep watch on every side, in the city itself and beyond the river.

This beautiful and evocative description of the city is made more poignant by the fate that it befell at the hands of Björn Ironside. When he had finished, Paris lay almost completely in ruins; only four churches were left standing. Filled with a horrible pride at the destruction they had wrought, Björn Ironside and Hastein decided that, having taken the greatest city in northern Europe, it surely would not be beyond their capabilities to take the greatest city in the world: Rome.

They took sixty-two ships, sailed back down the Seine, and made for the Bay of Biscay, stopping on the way only to pillage. When they reached Moorish Spain, their ships were full of gold, silver, and prisoners. They may have considered sacking Seville, but a skirmish with Moorish forces off the mouth of the Guadalquivir, which cost them two ships, made them think better of it, and instead they sailed through the Strait of Gibraltar into the Mediterranean.

They attacked and plundered Algeciras, sailed south to the coast of North Africa to pick up slaves (whom they later sold in Ireland), and then proceeded north to attack the Balearic Islands, Narbonne, and the Camargue. They spread terror along the Côte d'Azur and the coast of Liguria in northern Italy, before turning south, toward Rome.

Eventually they spied a fortified city whose marble walls glittered dazzling white in the sunlight. They gazed on the marvelous city with lustful, rapacious eyes, but were forced to concede that they would not be able to storm its great walls of gleaming white marble. Not content to leave empty-handed, they decided on one of the most audacious (not to

mention outrageous) schemes in history. Hastein sent messengers to the city to say that their chieftain was mortally ill,
and was desperate to be baptized before he died. The request
was granted, and Hastein was baptized. The following day,
his men returned to the city gates, crying that their chieftain
had died, and pleading for him to be given a Christian burial. This request also was granted, and, in the words of the
chronicler Dudo of St. Quentin (quoted in Magnusson):

> A clamour of wailing is heard, and tumultuous mourn-
> ing. The mountains reverberate, echoing the sound of
> deceitful grief. The bishop summons by bells the people
> throughout the whole city. The clergy came, dressed in
> monastic vestments. Similarly the chief men of the city
> came, soon to be crowned with martyrdom. The women
> came in throngs, soon to be led into exile. With one will
> they go to meet the monster laid on the bier. The schol-
> ars bear candles and crosses, walking before their seniors.

The plan worked perfectly. As the "dead" Hastein was
about to be lowered into his grave, he sprang up from the
bier and slew the officiating bishop with his sword. His men
drew their own weapons, which they had concealed beneath
their mourning cloaks, and opened the city gates for their
comrades waiting outside. The Vikings spilled into the city,
transforming the day into a hideous maelstrom of slaughter,
rape, and pillage.

The Vikings, however, made a serious error: the city they
had assumed was Rome was in fact a town called Luna, about
186 miles north of their intended target. When he realized his
mistake, Hastein was driven into a frenzy of rage. He took all
the prisoners he could for slaves, killed the rest, and burned
Luna to the ground.

This is quite a story, but how accurate is it? It is likely that
Hastein did sack Luna, but not under the mistaken impression that it was Rome. Magnusson writes:

[B]y no stretch of the imagination could any Viking leader have confused Luna with Rome. That can only have been a chronicler's elaboration, to put it mildly. Luna had certainly been a large and important city in Roman times, but by the middle of the ninth century it was in serious economic decline and by 1200 it would be abandoned completely. By Hastein's time the impressive Roman buildings of Carrara marble from the quarries nearby were all in ruins, the magnificent amphitheatre and the forum lying derelict, the town reduced to a scattered settlement with a fortified nucleus round its cathedral.

Today Luna is called Luni, and has been extensively excavated by archaeologists from the Centro di Studi Lunensi. In addition, a team of British and Italian archaeologists investigated the early medieval levels of the town but were unable to find any trace of the destruction said to have been visited on it by the Vikings. Although Hastein probably did sack the town, exactly what he did there is now lost to history.

Magnusson notes that, ironically, "the only certain Viking 'visiting card' in the area is to be found in a city which we know the Vikings never molested at all." On the shoulder of a huge marble lion that now guards the entrance to the old arsenal in Venice, there is a runic inscription, badly weathered and now indecipherable. The lion was not sculpted in Venice, but was seized by the Venetians during a military expedition to Greece in the late seventeenth century. The inscription was carved into the lion's shoulder by a Swedish Viking sometime in the late eleventh century, when the Viking Age was at an end. Magnusson concludes:

The Mediterranean had never really been for the Vikings. They were too far from their natural habitat. It is symbolic that the reason we cannot read these runes today is that they were not carved deeply enough on that proud lion from classical Greece. Time and trouble have helped to erode them, and only infra-red photography to divine the disturbed crystalline structure of the underlying marble might conceivably enable us to decipher them one day. But I doubt if we shall ever know. Like the runes on the . . . lion, the impact of the Vikings on the Mediterranean was simply too slight.

Weapons and Fortifications of the Warriors

The image of the Viking as a fearsome warrior descending like the wrath of an ancient god on his enemies is largely accurate. However, the picture many people have of the stereotypical Viking in a horned helmet has been proved completely wrong by the archaeological remains we have discovered. It is not entirely certain why the erroneous image of the horned helmet has gained such wide currency, but it may be due to the first representations of Wagner's operas, inspired by antique golden drinking horns discovered in Denmark in the seventeenth and eighteenth centuries. Unfortunately, those horns were stolen in 1802 and melted; the ones on display at the National Museum of Denmark are copies. Viking helmets were typically made of metal or leather, with a vertical bar to protect the nose. It was very difficult to move quickly and freely during close-quarters fighting, and horns sprouting from his helmet would have proved a dangerous inconvenience to a Viking warrior.

Throughout the Dark Ages, war and the possibility of violent death hung like a storm cloud on the horizon of people's lives. For a warrior people such as the Vikings, weapons and fighting tactics were of extreme importance. On the whole, precise details of combat during the Viking Age are rather sketchy; however, descriptions of some battles are preserved in the Icelandic sagas. According to the laws of the Scandinavian countries, every able-bodied man was required to possess weapons suitable to his social standing. In Norway the weapons of choice were a sword or ax, a spear, and a shield; in Sweden and Denmark an iron helmet was added to the list.

For wealthy Vikings, including the aristocracy, the sword was the weapon of choice. The blade usually was imported from Frankish workshops, with the hilt fitted locally and decorated with gold, silver, or copper. Swords usually were engraved with the maker's name, the most common being Ingelrii and Ulfberht. The blades were double-edged, about 3 feet long, and 4 inches wide at the base, tapering to a rounded tip. These weapons were used for slashing rather than thrusting, and were constructed by an ingenious method known as "pattern welding." The central section of the blade was fashioned from several iron rods that were twisted or plated together and then beaten into shape. The result was a blade that was strong and pliable, and much harder to break than traditional swords made from a single piece of metal. A harder edge was then welded to the core, leaving the pattern of the twisted rods visible in the blade. It was only later, when smelting technology improved, that pattern welding was gradually abandoned.

Another highly favored weapon was the ax, of which there were several varieties. The single-handed version was short and light and was used as a throwing weapon, a deadly projectile that could spin with lethal force through the tumult and confusion of a battle to find its mark. Its larger cousin, known as the Danish ax, was 3.3 to 4.9 feet long, and was wielded in two hands. The Danish ax was a truly fearsome weapon, capable of beheading a horse with a single stroke. It is best known from the scenes on the Bayeaux Tapestry in which King Harold's foot soldiers engage in hand-to-hand combat with the invading Normans. These foot soldiers, or housecarls, belonged to the household of an earl or king and were the best equipped and most experienced of his men. Usually they were deployed in the front line of a battle, their ferocity and proficiency acting as a powerful morale boost to their comrades. They also operated as highly mobile and fast-reacting units that could be directed at a moment's notice to reinforce areas weakened during the battle. It was the responsibility of the housecarls to defend the leader and his standard.

When Vikings were buried, their precious weapons were placed in the graves with them. Among the most common weapons found in Scandinavian graves during the early Viking Age are spears, and although the practice of burying weapons in graves disappeared with the conversion to Christianity, spears nevertheless remained the weapon most often used in battle. The reason is that they were cheap and easy to produce, and could be used to great effect with little or no training. Viking spearheads tended to be long and thin — 12 to 20 inches — and could be used either to thrust at an opponent or to slash at him. Some archaeologists suggest that spears could be used in combination with a shield; but from the reconstructed length of the shafts it is more likely that the spears were used without a shield and with two hands once the enemy had got too close to allow missiles to be used effectively. However, shorter spears also have been found, suggesting that once a battle had commenced, spears were thrown at the enemy prior to the lines closing.

Bows and arrows also were frequently used, both in hunting and fighting, especially at sea. The bows were made of yew or ash and were 3.3 to 6.6 feet long, with an effective range of 656 feet. At close range the arrows would certainly be able to pierce mail armor, but would be less effective at longer ranges. They were a deadly danger only to unarmored warriors.

Viking shields were traditionally made of lime wood, although the most common materials used were larch, beech, oak, and pine. Reinforced with leather or rawhide, they were quite thin, which gave them the advantage of being easy to wield, but which also meant that they would not last longer than a single battle. Throughout the Viking Age, shields were invariably round (although kite-shaped shields, giving greater protection to the legs, became common much later), and ranged from 2 to 4 feet in diameter. They had a circular hole cut in the center, covered with a conical or hemispherical iron boss, where the shield was gripped. The thinness of their construction strongly implies that they were used to deflect blows rather than to directly parry them; it is unlikely that a shield could have withstood the force of a sword or ax blow.

In battle, an adequate means of defense was at least as important as reliable weapons of attack, and Vikings tended to favor mail shirts, or *byrnie,* when going into battle. Viking mail was made from iron rings that were either punched from a single sheet or wound from a drawn wire. A typical mail shirt contained no fewer than thirty thousand rings. They were difficult and time-consuming to make and so, like the mail garments worn by the knights of Europe, were worn only by those who could afford them. Most mail shirts had half-length sleeves and reached either to the midthigh or the knee. Although they gave good protection to the most vulnerable parts of the warrior's body, they did not make him invulnerable. A slashing sword might be easily deflected, but the massive force of a two-handed ax blow could still crush bones and internal organs, rendering a warrior helpless and probably close to death. Likewise, a spear thrust with two hands would almost certainly be able to pierce the mail, and shorter spears would be equally dangerous if aimed at the face.

The Vikings' fearsome reputation arose from their battle tactics as much as from their skill and ferocity. Once a battle commenced, the opposing sides would form the "shield wall," a single line several warriors deep, with each warrior overlapping his shield with that of his neighbor to form a virtually impenetrable wall. Following the initial charge, the shield walls would break in places to allow individual combat. At this point in the battle, for the opponent to lose one's concentration even for a moment was to invite death from one of the many spears in use.

It was equally vital not to move back, for the enemy could take advantage of a retreat of even a few feet and ultimately win the day. Such close-quarters battles were vicious and desperate affairs, with swords, axes, spears, and arrows tracing lethal arcs of metal and blood through an atmosphere filled with the screams of the fighting and the dying. Even the greatest of warriors could find it almost impossible to maneuver effectively during close-quarters combat. It was therefore common for an army to attempt to outflank its opponent. (This is how Harald Hardradi's army was defeated at the Battle of Stamford Bridge.)

One of the most successful battle tactics used by the Vikings was the "Boar's Snout" or "Swine Array," said to have been taught to the Norsemen by their chief god, Odin. The Boar's Snout was basically a wedge-shaped charge aimed directly at the opposing side's shield wall. If timed properly, the Boar's Snout could throw the opposing army into panic and disarray as their massed ranks were split down the middle.

Viking leaders attained their position through skill and courage in battle. It was therefore expected that the leader would lead from the front, standing more or less at the center of the front line, leading the charge or the Boar's Snout. As a result, the course of the battle was likely to follow the fortunes of the leaders: if a leader was cut down, his army probably would withdraw and concede defeat (his housecarls were expected to remain with him and die, if necessary). It therefore made sense for a Viking leader to seek out his opposite number as quickly as possible and kill him, thus ensuring a swift victory.

While the Vikings' reputation as superb and ruthless warriors was richly deserved, it was based partly on the activities of a certain group whose very name has come to mean a violent loss of sanity: the Berserkers. The word "berserker" is of uncertain origin, and may derive from "bare-sark," meaning a warrior who fought without armor, or "bear-sark," meaning a warrior dressed in animal skins. The Berserkers were truly terrifying, and were regarded with awe even by their fellow Vikings. They fought like wild animals on the battlefield and sometimes are described as wolves in the sagas. It was said that when fighting they were possessed by the souls of animals and were virtually invulnerable to the enemy's weapons. The belief in their invulnerability was well founded, for such was their battle frenzy that they ignored the pain of their wounds and continued to fight on regardless, even when those wounds ultimately proved to be fatal. Their appearance was calculated to inspire terror in their foes; they painted their faces to give themselves the appearance of creatures that were part man and part animal — an appearance that may have contributed to the rise of the werewolf legend in Europe.

The mental state of these individuals during battle was known as *berserkergang*. To face them was to find oneself confronting men whose rational minds had been obliterated by an animalistic lust for blood and whose strength was double that of even the strongest warrior. They slaughtered every living thing they encountered, unable even to distinguish between friends and enemies. It is believed that the Berserkers reached this mental state through the ingestion of large quantities of alcohol, and perhaps hallucinogenic mushrooms, although this is by no means proven.

Berserkergang also could occur during hard physical labor, and the men who were seized with it displayed astonishing strength. It is said to have begun with shivering and chattering of teeth, followed by swelling and discoloration of the face. The man would then be consumed with uncontrollable rage, and would scream and howl like a wild animal. He would bite down on the edge of his shield, and would become unstoppable in his mindless desire to kill. When the Berserker returned to his senses, he became suddenly extremely weak and dull of mind, a condition that would persist for several days. Some Berserkers even died from exhaustion following a battle.

Such was the violence and cruelty exhibited by the Berserkers that they were not liked by their fellow Vikings. In fact, they were frequently shunned by the community, and compelled to live alone, far from their fellows. In 1015 a law was passed making it illegal to be a Berserker, with a penalty of three years' banishment from the country.

The Vikings also needed to defend their lands and towns from attack and capture, and they did this chiefly through the construction of ramparts, fortresses, and sea barriers. The ramparts around the Danish market town of Hedeby offer one of the best examples of this type of defense. Hedeby (from the German *Haithabu,* "the place on the moor") was the southernmost town in Scandinavia, lying on the eastern side of the Jutland Peninsula near modern-day Schleswig. Its proximity to the border with the Frisians, Saxons, and Slavs ensured its importance as a center of international trade. However, its wealth also ensured the need for an adequate means of defense.

The earliest settlement dates from the eighth century, and the town is first referred to in the Frankish Annals of A.D. 804. Thereafter, Hedeby is mentioned many times in various sources, including foreign writings, on rune stones, and in poetry. Thanks to extensive excavations of the site in the 1930s and 1960s, which turned up thousands of artifacts, we know much about the town and the way of life within its walls. It was a busy place, its inhabitants mingling with visiting merchants on wood-paved streets running between workshops, warehouses, and barns. There was a Craftsmen's Quarter in which lived jewelers, smiths, leatherworkers, carpenters, and many other makers of valuable merchandise. The town even boasted the first mint in Scandinavia. Aside from the goods manufactured there, Hedeby also was a center for trade in goods from far-off lands, including slaves from the Baltic, wine and weapons from other parts of western Europe, and furs from the icy lands of the Far North. Hedeby also was the location of the first Christian church in Denmark, which was built in about 850.

Hedeby was built around a stream running from west to east. Its streets either followed the direction of the river or ran perpendicular to it. On each side of the streets stood small, fenced-in plots, each containing a rectangular house roughly 33 feet long and 16.5 feet wide. Some of these plots also contained an outhouse and a well.

The Frankish Annals of the year 808 relate how the Danish king Godfred destroyed a Slav trading station called Reric, and moved the merchants from there to Hedeby. The semicircular wall surrounding the town and facing inland is 0.8 mile long and up to 36 feet high. It was built in the midtenth century, and is linked by the connecting wall to the Danevirke (Danish Work), the massive series of fortifications built across the base of the Jutland Peninsula between the North Sea and the Baltic. The earthworks of the Danevirke were erected at various times for the defense of Jutland and were frequently rebuilt and strengthened. Dendrochronology (tree-ring dating) conducted in the 1970s established that work on the Danevirke began as early as the 730s, undermining the previous consensus that King Godfred had been responsible for the first ramparts.

As Hedeby grew in importance, its fortifications were strengthened, including the forewall and a system of deep ditches. At the height of its prosperity the town had a population of a thousand to fifteen hundred. Excavations of the site have not revealed any royal residences; however, examinations of Hedeby's cemeteries show that there were considerable differences in class. The inhabitants of the town houses were buried in simple graves; but there also are chamber graves, including the "boat-chamber grave" containing swords, riding equipment, and many other goods.

Hedeby was sacked more than once in the eleventh century (Harald Hardradi of Norway conquered it in 1050), and by 1100 it lay abandoned. As Hedeby declined, nearby Schleswig grew in importance, not least because its location allowed easier access to the deeper-drafted merchant ships being developed at the time.

The fortifications of towns such as Hedeby, Ribe, Birka, and Århus were semicircular and faced inland. Another form of fortification used in Denmark was the trelleborg, named after the fortress on the western coast of Sjælland. Four of these were military encampments: Trelleborg, Nonnebakken on the island of Fyn, Fyrkat in eastern Jutland, and Aggersborg (the largest) in northern Jutland. Each of these precisely planned and constructed fortresses had a circular rampart reinforced with internal timbers, with a sloping outer wall faced with wood. They had four gateways positioned at the points of the compass, and were divided into quadrants by two timber-paved streets crossing at right angles at the center. Within each quadrant stood four timber buildings arranged in the shape of a square. The rampart was surrounded by a v-shaped ditch.

It is by no means clear exactly what these constructions were used for: it seems that they had been in use for no longer than twenty or thirty years, and their excavation revealed very few artifacts. Likewise, the absence of weapons leads Magnus Magnusson to comment that either "they had been barracks which had been kept scrupulously tidy by the soldiers; or . . . they had not been barracks at all." Magnusson continues in *The Vikings:*

Many scholars have concluded that they *must* have been barracks, built specifically for invasion purposes; and since the only major invasion undertaken by Denmark which we know about was the invasion of England by Harald Blue-Tooth's son, Svein Fork-Beard, in 1013 . . . it was assumed that they must have been built by Svein Fork-Beard for that purpose.

The new dendrochronological dating from Trelleborg destroyed that assumption. Preliminary reports of dendro-dates from Fyrkat, suggesting the year 976, seem to confirm Trelleborg's dating. It looks very much as if all the four "Trelleborgs" were built by Harald Blue-Tooth, and not during the reign of his son, King Svein Fork-Beard.

Magnusson concludes that if this is true, it can only mean that Harald Blue-Tooth built them as barracks to consolidate his own power over Denmark and to guard against the volatility of his subjects. This volatility had several causes, including an acute shortage of silver; the Danes' defeat at the Danevirke in 974; their loss of supremacy over Norway and the drastic decrease in tributes; and Harald Blue-Tooth's construction of many large buildings through the imposition of public labor duties.

There is evidence that villages were demolished to make way for construction of the fortresses of Trelleborg and Aggersborg; and at Trelleborg, several wells were discovered containing the bodies of children. Within the fortresses themselves, of course, nothing remains of the timber from which the buildings had been constructed. We can only make educated guesses as to the layout from the dark patches that remain, combined with our knowledge of the building customs of the age.

Although they were barracks, the trelleborgs housed women, children, and craftsmen as well as soldiers. It is likely that the fortresses performed other functions as well as housing warriors: they were regional centers of royal power and administration. The huge fortress of Aggersborg seems to have been intended for a special role. It was situated near the northern tip of Jutland, thus giving easy access to Norway, where Harald Blue-Tooth had a number of important interests. In addition, he could collect tolls on the north–south road through the peninsula, and on the shipping through the Limfjord between western Europe and the Baltic.

Throughout Scandinavia, defenses were erected to provide protection against attacks from the sea. The harbors at Hedeby and Birka contained sharpened wooden stakes, as did the fjords and bays leading to other settlements. In addition, the approaches to settlements were blocked by large stones and even scuttled ships, which formed a kind of maze that only those with local knowledge would be able to navigate. These defenses also were used elsewhere in Europe, as a means of preventing Viking raiders from traveling along rivers to reach their targets. Of course, these water defenses could be as hazardous for the local population as for the attackers, especially in the sea, whose waves and currents could dash any ship against the hidden obstacles.

Although overshadowed by the Battle of Hastings, which occurred three weeks later, the Battle of Stamford Bridge was among the most significant in the history of the British Isles, since it was the last Viking battle to be fought on English soil and marked the effective end of the Viking Era in English history.

Edward the Confessor was king of the English from 1042 to 1066. Son of Aethelred the Unready (c. 968–1016) and later stepson of Knut, Edward spent much of his time in religious work, including construction of Westminster Abbey. Since he had no heirs, his death would begin a three-way rivalry for the English throne that would ultimately see the end of Anglo-Saxon rule in England. In 1066, while on his deathbed, the king summoned his Witen, or advisory council, and commended his kingdom and the protection of his queen to Harold Godwinson, earl of Wessex. Harold was the second most powerful man in the country, and a close adviser to and brother-in-law of the king. His closeness to the king, combined with the esteem in which he was held by his peers, meant that Harold was the logical choice as successor to the throne. Following Edward's deathbed endorsement, the Witan had no hesitation in selecting Harold as king.

Across the English Channel, Duke William of Normandy also had designs on the English throne. He justified his claim through the fact that he and Edward were distantly related, and his insistence that some years earlier, Edward had designated him successor.

While Duke William of Normandy was waiting for favorable winds to carry his invasion force across the English Channel, the Norwegians, led by Harald Hardradi (whose name meant "hard ruler"), sailed across the North Sea by way of the Orkney Islands to Scotland, where he joined Earl

Tostig, the English king's brother. Among Hardradi's invasion force were men from Denmark, Sweden, Iceland, Greenland, the Faeroes, Orkney, the Isle of Man, and northern Scotland.

The same winds that prevented William of Normandy from crossing the Channel took Hardradi and Tostig south along the eastern coast of England, until they landed and attacked the town of Scarborough on September 15, 1066. News of the attack reached Harold in London within a week, and he decided he had little choice but to head north to meet the invasion head-on, before returning quickly to the south to guard against the Norman threat of invasion. Having put Scarborough to the torch, Hardradi and Tostig sailed up the Humber and Ouse Rivers to Ricall, where Hardradi moored his fleet. He then led his forces toward York, where the earls of Northumbria and Mercia were waiting for them with their own hastily assembled forces.

The armies met on September 20 at Fulford on the Ouse, where the English army blocked the roads and rivers, with their flanks protected by marshes. The young and inexperienced earls acquitted themselves admirably in the long and bloody battle that followed. There were successes and failures on each side, but eventually Hardradi won the day. Although the earls escaped with their lives, there were many dead on the English side. Hardradi, too, had lost many men, and he lost no time in making for York, where he demanded supplies and a hundred hostages to ensure that the city's people were obedient to him. The hostages were to be handed to him at Stamford Bridge, which spanned the Derwent River, on September 25.

Harold set out for Yorkshire on September 20. He had an army of approximately six thousand, half of which was made up of his housecarls and half of local militia (the Select Fyrd) he recruited or pressed into service on the way. He covered an impressive 50 miles per day to arrive at Tadcaster, about 10 miles southwest of York, on September 24. Having stationed guards at all the entrances to Tadcaster and other strategic points on the way to York, to ensure that knowledge of his presence in Yorkshire was kept from Hardradi and Tostig, Harold allowed his men to rest and recuperate from their march northward while he continued to gather intelligence on his enemies' movements.

King Harold met with the English survivors of the battle at Fulford on the Ouse, who told him that Hardradi and Tostig had already left York and returned to their fleet, which was moored at Riccall on the Ouse. From people who had been in York when it surrendered he learned one other vital piece of information: the place at which the hostages and supplies were to be transferred the following day.

Harold quickly decided on his best course of action: he would first go to York to reestablish his authority there (the Norwegians had neglected to leave a garrison in the city); then he would take his army to Stamford Bridge and surprise the Viking forces there. A direct attack on Riccall was out of the question, since they would have been spotted by Viking sentries. According to *The Anglo-Saxon Chronicle,* King Harold's forces departed Tadcaster early on the morning of Monday, September 25, and rode the 10 miles to York. From there they rode the remaining 8 miles to Stamford Bridge, keeping to the Roman road for the first 7 miles, then halting at Helmsley Gate. There they waited, just out of sight of Stamford Bridge, for the Vikings to arrive.

Hardradi's men duly arrived and, not expecting to face any resistance, leisurely assembled in groups on each side of the Derwent to await the arrival of their hostages and supplies. Instead, they were greeted with the sight of Harold's army charging toward them over the hill to the south. The day was hot, and Hardradi had allowed his men to divest themselves of their armor and helmets, a mistake that was to cost the Vikings dearly. In addition, he had left a third of his army at Riccall to guard the fleet. Tostig urged Hardradi to retreat to Riccall, but Hardradi decided to accept battle: Harold, he believed, would surely have sent part of his army ahead to block such a retreat, and it was almost certain that the English king's housecarls would rapidly close in on the Vikings' flank if they attempted to make for their fleet.

Hardradi thus decided to face Harold in battle, and sent a messenger back to Riccall to alert Eystein Orri, the commander of the contingent there, to bring his men to Stamford Bridge as quickly as possible. The battle for the bridge itself was short-lived. In spite of the Vikings' efforts (in particular, those of an anonymous Norseman who held the bridge alone, killing more than forty men with his battle-ax until he was stabbed from beneath with a long spear), they could not hold the bridge and were forced to retreat to a ridge overlooking the river.

They formed a shield wall in the shape of a triangle, to present a narrow front to Harold's men. The king immediately ordered them to charge. The fighting was fierce and bloody and lasted much of the day, but in the end Harold's housecarls prevailed. Harald Hardradi took an arrow in the throat and was killed, which was a disaster for his men, as the Icelandic court poet Thjodolf Arnarsson wrote:

Disaster has befallen us;
I say the army has been duped.
There was no cause for Harald
To bring his forces westward.
Mighty Harald is fallen
And we are all imperilled;
Norway's renowned leader
Has lost his life in England.

Tostig tried in vain to rally the Norsemen, who were utterly demoralized by the death of their leader. He also fell during the battle. Even the arrival of Eystein Orri with reinforcements could not turn the tide for the Vikings, not least because the march from Riccall had exhausted them.

His victory now assured, King Harold pursued the fleeing Vikings back to their fleet at Riccall, easily overwhelming them as they desperately and valiantly attempted to defend themselves and their ships. The few surviving Vikings surrendered. There were only enough left of them to man twenty-four of the nearly three hundred ships in the fleet. Harold permitted them to take their dead with them back to Norway, including the body of their leader, Harald Hardradi. Tostig's body was later buried in York.

The Battle of Stamford Bridge, at which Harold made good his promise to give Hardradi "seven feet of English soil," effectively ended the Viking threat to England. It was a splendid victory for King Harold and the Saxons. Their celebrations, however, were short-lived, for news arrived that Duke William of Normandy had landed near Hastings. With barely time to catch their breath after the fierce battle they had just fought, they turned south and marched down to the southern coast of England as quickly as they had marched north to Yorkshire.

Although his victory at Stamford Bridge had secured Harold's position against the threat from the Norsemen, Duke William of Normandy constituted the greater threat. William, also known as William the Bastard, was the illegitimate son of Duke Robert I of Normandy, who declared William his successor despite his illegitimacy. Having grown up with his Great-Uncle Robert, archbishop of Rouen, and his Uncle Walter as his protectors, he prevailed against challenges from his cousin, Guy of Burgundy, Count Geoffrey of Anjou, and King Henry of France. William gradually consolidated his political and military strength, and by the time King Philip I ascended to the French throne, William had married Mathilda of Flanders, the daughter of Philip's guardian.

Having learned that William had landed at Pevensey, King Harold took his already battle-weary soldiers south to meet this new threat, only stopping at London for reinforcements. He then continued south to Caldbec Hill, a few miles north of Hastings, where William had positioned his own forces. The solid ground in this area was interrupted by ravines, streams, and patches of marshland. In positioning his army at the summit of Caldbec Hill, Harold not only had a clear view of the enemy but also had blocked the only route out of the Hastings area, forcing the Normans into an uphill attack. Harold built a shield wall along Sentlache Ridge, of which Caldbec Hill forms a part. He placed his housecarls and thegns, who were skilled fighters, between his fyrdmen, who were less skilled. His initial strategy was to wait for the Normans to attack, hoping that the uphill assault would tire them out and allow him to counterattack with relative ease.

Although Harold had an apparent tactical advantage at the summit of Caldbec Hill, William showed considerable shrewdness in deciding to land at Pevensey, which was on a lagoon and thus provided shelter from the weather. His five hundred ships also could be beached high on the land at high tide. Unfortunately for Harold, the troops he had deployed along the southern coast and the Isle of Wight several weeks earlier had grown demoralized while waiting for action, and were deeply concerned about the harvest waiting to be gathered at their homes. Harold disbanded them at the beginning of September, and lost many of his ships in the same storm that had delayed William's departure from Normandy. This, combined with the fatigue suffered by his troops following their rapid march from the north, meant that he was woefully ill prepared to meet the second invasion force in as many weeks.

William's army, which numbered six thousand to seven thousand troops, including about two thousand cavalry, was divided into three sections: the left section was composed mainly of Bretons; the center contained mainly Normans, and was under William's direct command; and the right section was composed of French and Flemish. Each of these sections was further subdivided into three rows of archers, infantry, and cavalry. William's strategy was that of a three-pronged attack, commencing with the archers letting fly their arrows to pick off as many Saxons as possible, followed by the infantry, who would engage the enemy in hand-to-hand combat, with the cavalry finally bringing up the rear to crush whoever remained.

The Battle of Hastings began early on the morning of Saturday, October 14, 1066, with the Norman archers raining their arrows on the Saxon shield wall. However, as the infantry and cavalry moved up for the attack, Harold's men offered such violent resistance that the members of the Breton contingent, who were less experienced than their comrades, were thrown into panic and confusion. Failing to keep in line with the other sections, they raced blindly ahead, saw that they were dangerously exposed, and immediately began to retreat. Seeing this, the less experienced among the Saxon forces rushed down the hill after them but were caught by the Normans and killed.

William continued with his plan of attack, charging at the Saxons along with his cavalry. As the day wore on and each side suffered appalling casualties, William saw that his army's supply of arrows was running low, so he ordered his archers to fire them high into the air, so that their trajectories would take them deeper into the Saxon lines. The sudden change in strategy worked superbly, causing even more casualties and the eventual collapse of the Saxon shield wall. The Normans took full advantage of the collapse of their enemies' defenses and mounted a catastrophic penetration of their ranks. King Harold received a fatal (and now legendary) wound from an arrow through his face, and his men, their morale now completely undermined by the death of their leader, were routed by the Normans.

William went on to capture Canterbury, Winchester, and London, and was crowned king on Christmas Day 1066, beginning an eighty-eight-year period of Norman rule in England. The results of William's victory at the Battle of Hastings were of immense significance for England. Not only was the Norman feudal system introduced, but also Anglo-Saxon freedom and rights were seriously curtailed. However, her ties with Normandy ensured that England would become a powerful player in European politics. In 1085 William ordered a comprehensive survey of English landholdings, which resulted in the *Domesday Book,* so called because it was thought to be as authoritative as the Last Judgment.

Dragons of the Sea

The Viking lives on in our imaginations as a powerful symbol of the sea; and there is no more potent symbol of the Viking than the longship. This vessel, which was also called a "dragon ship" by those upon whom the Vikings descended in their Europe-wide raids, was the medieval equivalent of a modern troop carrier. They were large and sleek, possessing a terrible grace that struck fear into the hearts of all who witnessed their arrival. The average longship was 92 feet long and carried a crew of twenty to thirty oarsmen; a helmsman, who steered the ship; a lookout, who kept his eyes peeled for dangerous rocks in shallow waters; and several men who could step in when an oarsman was tired, or was lost overboard in rough seas.

We know a great deal about the design, construction, and uses of Viking ships from the many vessels and fragments of vessels that have survived. Without doubt, the most famous and well-preserved Viking ships are the Norwegian burial ships from Gokstad (excavated in 1880) and Oseberg (excavated in 1904). Dendrochronology (the dating of the ships by examining the tree rings on their wooden hulls) has shown that the burial of the Gokstad ship took place in about 900–905, and the Oseberg ship in about 834. In 1962, five shipwrecks were excavated in Roskilde Fjord in Denmark at Skuldelev; these ships, known now as Skuldelev 1–5, were originally scuttled to block the fjord. These are the most famous Viking ship finds, although many other vessels were sunk in harbors as underwater defensive screens.

Viking longships were incredibly beautiful and elegant vessels, and that beauty and elegance are preserved in the examples that have survived. Although there were a number of variations on the basic design (which will be described later), we can take the Gokstad ship as a standard on which to base a description of their appearance and construction. The keel of the Gokstad ship was 57 feet, 9 inches long and was made from a single oak timber. She was 76 feet, 6 inches long, with a beam of 17 feet, 6 inches, and was just over 6 feet, 4 inches from the bottom of the keel to the gunwale amidships. She was clinker-built (or lapstraked) of sixteen strakes, with the waterline strake 1.75 inches thick, and the nine strakes below the waterline and the three above 1 inch thick. The oar strake was 1.25 inches thick, and the two topmost strakes were 0.88 inch.

The Oseberg ship is nearly 71 feet long, with a beam of 16 feet. There are beautiful spiral terminals at the prow and stern, and the leading edge and uppermost strakes are decorated with complex animal shapes.

In his comprehensive study *A History of the Vikings,* Gwyn Jones gives a concise yet detailed description of the ship's construction:

The strakes were joined together by round-headed iron rivets driven through from the outside and secured inside by means of small square iron plates. The caulking was of tarred animal hair or wool. The hull was kept in shape by nineteen frames and crossbeams. The decking of pine, in this case loose so that the space beneath could be used for storage, was laid over these beams. The strakes below the waterline were tied to the frame with spruce root lashings (in the Oseberg ship with narrow strips of whalebristle . . .), a device which contributed much to the ship's flexibility. This was still further increased by a carefully systematized trenailing of the above-water strakes to wooden knees and crossbeams or, in the case of the top two, to half-ribs secured to the strakes below and butted into the underside of the gunwale.

The elasticity of this part of the ship was such that the replica of the Gokstad ship sailed across the Atlantic in 1893 by Magnus Andersen (a twenty-eight day passage from Bergen [Norway] to Newfoundland) showed a gunwale twisting out of true by as much as 6 inches, yet was safe, fast, and watertight. With her mighty keel and flexible frame and planking the Viking ship was an inspired combination of strength and elasticity. And this power to cross seas and oceans did not exhaust her excellence as a raider. An exceedingly shallow draught, rarely exceeding 3½ feet, allowed her to penetrate all save the shallowest rivers, gave her mastery of harbourless shelving beaches, and facilitated the rapid disembarkation of men at the point of attack. By turning into the wind and making off by oar she was almost immune from pursuit by the clumsier sailing-ships of the lands she preyed on.

The ship was constructed mainly of oak, and the sixteen pairs of oars were of pine, as was the approximately 30-foot-tall mast. The rectangular sail, approximately 23 by 36 feet, was made of strips of heavy woolen cloth and seems to have been strengthened by a network of ropes. The mast was secured in a very large and robust structure known as the "old woman" *(kerling)* or keelson, which was a solid block of oak resting on the keel over four frames. The keelson had a large socket into which the mast fitted. Above the keelson lay the mast partner, another enormous block of oak, with a solid forward section and a grooved rear section, to allow the mast to be lowered. Gwyn Jones writes:

> From the Gotland pictorial stones it appears that the sail could be effectively shortened by the use of reefing lines, and recent opinion has inclined to the view that the Viking ship could be sailed across and even near the wind. This was largely due to the use of the *beitiáss,* a removable pole or tacking boom whose heavy end was

seated in a socket abeam of the mast while its lighter end was fitted to the forward leech of the sail to keep it taut and drawing when the ship was sailing on the wind.

The ship was steered by means of a side rudder attached to the starboard quarter. *Stýra,* to steer, is the origin of the word "starboard," meaning the right-hand side. A small ship's boat would often be carried on board or towed behind. Three of these smaller boats were found with the Gokstad ship, although Gwyn Jones suggests that two of them may not be true ship's boats but grave goods. At night, a tent was raised on deck for sleeping quarters. Although we tend to think of the Viking longship as being rowed toward its target, it was primarily a sailing ship; oars were used only when the vessel was becalmed or required careful maneuvering along rivers or fjords.

Perhaps the most important questions about the Oseberg and Gokstad ships are the identities of the people buried in them. Oseberg contained the bodies of two women, one old and one young; and Gokstad contained the remains of a man. These are very difficult questions to answer, but a clue may be found in Snorri Sturluson's *Heimskringla,* which chronicles the Yngling line of kings of Vestfold in Norway. We can pick up the story with Gudrød the Hunting King, the son of King Halfdan the Generous but Stingy with Food.

When his wife died, Gudrød set his sights on a young princess in the neighboring kingdom of Agder. Her name was Ása, and she was the daughter of King Harald Red-Beard of Agder. When his proposal of marriage was refused, Gudrød decided he would have to claim his prize the hard way, and sent warships to Agder. Ása's father and brother were killed, and the princess was carried off to be Gudrød's unwilling bride. Ása bore a son named Halfdan the Black, who would become the father of Harald Fine-Hair.

Gudrød paid dearly for his actions, for a year after the boy's birth, Ása had him murdered, and then returned to her own kingdom of Agder, where she ruled as queen mother and regent. Back in Vestfold, the throne passed to Gudrød's son, Ólaf Geirstada-Álf, a brave warrior, tall and handsome, with a superb physique. When Halfdan the Black reached age eighteen, he took over the kingdom of Agder from his mother, and then sent word to his half brother Ólaf, demanding his paternal inheritance, which amounted to half the kingdom of Vestfold. Ólaf seems to have agreed without too many complaints. This settlement gave to Halfdan new lands and the power necessary to launch several campaigns against neighboring territories.

Magnus Magnusson suggests that if this is an accurate rendering of history, then Gudrød's murder must have taken place in about the year 840, with Halfdan the Black succeeding to the throne of Agder in about 860. Magnusson continues in *The Vikings:*

> Ólaf Geirstada-Álf died, according to *Heimskringla,* of a disease of the leg, and was buried in a mound at Geirstadir. The superficial similarity of the names "Geirstadir" and "Gokstad" (earlier "Gjekstad") is tempting. Also, the first anatomical examination of the Gokstad skeleton indicated a well-built man in his fifties who had suffered severely from arthritis in the left knee and ankle: the "leg disease" of the saga? At the time that the Gokstad ship was interred, around 880 it is now thought, Ólaf Geirstada-Álf would have been about sixty years old. If the date and the medical evidence are correct, there is nothing inconsistent with the theory that Gokstad housed the mortal remains of Ólaf Geirstada-Álf.

Following Halfdan's succession, Queen Ása disappears from the saga, and we read nothing more of her, although it is likely that she went to Vestfold with her son. The Oseberg ship was intended to be the final resting place of a queen, and the similarity between "Ása" and "Oseberg" suggests that the ship may indeed have been her tomb. Even if this is true, the question remains: Which of the two female skeletons in the Oseberg ship is that of Queen Ása, the older or the younger?

Shortly after the funeral, grave robbers broke into the ship and dragged the two bodies out of the burial chamber at the center of the vessel. It is possible that the older woman was wearing precious bracelets and rings, for her right hand and left upper arm are missing. If this is the reason for the absence of the older woman's limbs, it implies that she was the queen, and the younger woman a servant who had either chosen or been ordered to die with her mistress, so that she might continue to serve her in the afterlife.

There are problems with this interpretation, however: the Gokstad man and the older Oseberg woman died at roughly the same age, give or take ten years or so; but the Oseberg burial is believed by many scholars to have taken place about sixty-six to seventy-one years earlier than Gokstad. If this is true, then the younger of the two female skeletons must be that of Queen Ása (assuming either of them is). Magnusson notes that this conclusion is based on examination of the different decorative styles employed in the burials, and adds that "not every scholar believes that relative dating on stylistic grounds can be so precise; the gap between the two burials . . . could have been as little as ten or fifteen years — which would be compatible with a fifty-year-old Queen Ása in Oseberg and a sixty-year-old King Ólaf in Gokstad."

During the 1950s and 1960s, advances in the science of underwater archaeology allowed the examination of many Viking vessels in situ, which led to a greater understanding of the many types that were built. The general name for a Viking warship was *skúta, snekkja, skeið, dreki* (dragonhead), and, of course the generic term *langskip* (longship). Some of these vessels were of an impressive size: Ólaf Tryggvason's *Long Serpent* was said to have thirty-four oars on each side, and Knut was said to possess a longship with sixty benches.

The five Skuldelev ships, however, are more representative of Viking ship dimensions. Now displayed at the Viking Ship

Museum in Roskilde, they were scuttled in the channel by Roskilde in about the year 1000 as a means of defense. Skuldelev 2 is a longship twenty-nine meters long and just over four meters wide, and probably carried a crew of fifty to sixty men; Skuldelev 5 also is a warship, but is smaller, with a length of just under seventeen and a half meters and a beam of just over two and a half meters. These ships were of the type used in Viking raids in Scandinavia, the Baltic, and western Europe.

In her book *The Vikings,* Else Roesdahl quotes a superbly evocative eleventh-century passage written by a monk from the monastery of St. Omer in Flanders regarding Viking ships and fleets. He is describing, in breathlessly enthusiastic terms, the invasion fleet of Svein Fork-Beard, which set sail from Denmark to England in 1013:

When at length they were all gathered, they went on board the towered ships, having picked out by observation each man his own leader on the brazen prows. On one side lions moulded in gold were to be seen on the ships, on the other birds on the tops of the masts indicated by their movements the winds as they blew, or dragons of various kinds poured fire from their nostrils. Here there were glittering men of solid gold or silver nearly comparable to live ones, there bulls with necks raised high and legs outstretched were fashioned leaping and roaring like live ones. One might see dolphins moulded in electrum, and centaurs in the same metal, recalling the ancient fable. In addition I might describe to you many examples of the same celature [embossing], if the names of the monsters which were there fashioned were known to me. But why should I now dwell upon the sides of the ships, which were not only painted with ornate colours but were covered with gold and silver figures? The royal vessel excelled the others in beauty as much as the king preceded the soldiers in the honour of his proper dignity, concerning which it is better that I be silent than that I speak inadequately. Placing their confidence in such a fleet, when the signal was suddenly given, they set out gladly, and, as they had been ordered, placed themselves round about the royal vessel with level prows, some [to starboard] and some [to port]. The blue water, smitten by many oars, might be seen foaming far and wide, and the sunlight, cast back in the gleam of metal, spread a double radiance in the air.

Skuldelev 3, built of oak, was 44 by 11 feet; and Skuldelev 1, built mainly of pine, was 54 by 15 feet. Both of these were deep-sea cargo carriers. The pine-built Skuldelev 1 was probably constructed in western Norway, and was one of the *knerrir* (singular, knörr) that sailed the Iceland–Greenland–Vinland route. She had an open hold amidships and half decks fore and aft, and probably was able to carry a cargo of about 20 tons.

Cargo ships were markedly different from their warship cousins: the former were much higher and wider in relation to their length, and their masts were fixed and could not be easily raised and lowered. They had fewer oars (the oar ports being above the half decks fore and aft), which were used only in narrow channels and to perform more complex maneuvers. Among the Viking Age cargo ships that have so far been discovered are the Klåstad ship, found near the trading center of Kaupang in Norway, and the Äskekärr ship, discovered near the mouth of the Göta River in Sweden. Both ships date from the tenth century.

Two full-size replicas were built of the Skuldelev cargo carriers, the *Saga Siglar* and the *Roar Ege*. From these ships, archaeologists have been able to ascertain the draft of the originals both loaded and unloaded, as well as the number of crew they required. It is clear that these ships were not suitable for routine river navigation (since they have very few oars). On certain routes, such as along the rivers of Russia, they had to be small and light enough to be carried short distances over land (Skuldelev 3 probably weighed about 2 tons).

A number of trials have been conducted with replica Viking ships, and these show that the originals were capable of speeds of 6 to 8 knots in favorable wind conditions. A speed of 10 knots maintained over 6 hours has been claimed for *Saga Siglar,* while *Roar Ege* had a maximum speed of 9 knots.

The Vikings' normal sailing procedure was to make their way along the coast during the day, and to make landfall and go ashore at night. However, they often sailed for several days without a break. We know very little about the way Vikings navigated on their arduous ocean voyages. What seems clear enough is that they must have based their navigation techniques on careful observation of their environment, including the behavior of seabirds, waves, and the positions of the sun and stars.

For long voyages, including those across the Atlantic, the Viking had the same problem as every mariner throughout history: how to fix one's latitude. Although we know that the Vikings were able to do this, we are not entirely sure how. Gwyn Jones writes in *A History of the Vikings:*

> We read, for example, of a detailed set of tables attrib-
> uted to the Icelander Star-Oddi, which gave the sun's
> midday latitude week by week throughout the year, as
> he observed this in northern Iceland towards the end of
> the tenth century. This or similar information recorded
> on so simple an object as a marked stick would give the
> mariner an indication of his then latitude as compared
> with a known place. Any observation of the midday sun,
> or if need be of the Pole Star, even by so crude a method
> as the measurement of a shadow cast at noon or the
> calculation of the Star's height above the horizon ex-
> pressed in terms of one's own arm, hand, or thumb, was
> a fair guide to latitude, which in the western voyages was
> much more important than longitude.

The reason for the importance of latitude over longitude was that, should a mariner be blown off course and become lost, he merely had to make for his correct latitude and then head in his desired direction to reach his intended destination. It is possible that Viking mariners were able to get their bearings through the use of wooden bearing dials or sun compasses, although the archaeological evidence for this is rather slight. The only indication that they used such instruments is half of a disc marked with equidistant notches, which was discovered by C. L. Vebaek in 1948 at Siglufjord in Greenland's Eastern Settlement. The half disc had a hole at its center, which could have held a shaft and shadow pin to indicate course. Although not all historians accept that this is actually part of a bearing dial, Gwyn Jones comments that it is hard to see what else it could be.

2

Gods and Monsters

All the champions
every day
contend in Odin's courtyard;
they choose the slain
and ride from the field,
thenceforth sit reconciled.
— Snorri Sturluson, *The Prose Edda*

The Creation of the World

We have already seen how the image of the Vikings as mindless barbarians dripping with blood is misleading and incomplete. In this chapter we will try to redress another misconception regarding the Norse people: that they were all pagans, with a vehement hatred of Christianity. It is perhaps understandable how this erroneous image arose in the popular imagination; after all, the Vikings were not at first a Christian people, and they certainly mounted many violent and bloody raids on Christian churches. However, the consensus among historians today is that the raids had little or nothing to do with religion: the churches and monasteries were attacked simply because they were wealthy and poorly defended — an irresistible combination for the Vikings. In addition, the Vikings were indeed pagans and worshiped many gods; as a result, they had no difficulty in accepting the existence of the Christian deity and incorporating it into their own religious system.

We can see from the archaeological evidence that when Vikings settled in Christian lands, such as the British Isles and Normandy, they swiftly adopted Christianity. It was normal practice for pagans to bury their dead with various items they would need in the afterlife. This is not, of course, a practice followed in Christianity, and the absence of these grave goods in Viking graves allows us to pinpoint the change in religion. Conversion to Christianity did not occur only in Viking colonies, but also in Scandinavia itself. By the middle of the eleventh century, Anglo-Saxon missionaries had seen to it that Christianity was well established in Denmark and much of Norway. There was a temporary conversion in Sweden at about the same time, but Christianity did not become fully established there until the middle of the twelfth century.

Although we know very little about the pagan religious practices of the Vikings beyond the fact that their leaders often functioned as priests, we have a great deal of information regarding their gods, goddesses, and other supernatural beings. The main sources are the Eddas, ancient folk tales that tell of the deeds of the old gods in the distant past. Interestingly, Christianity had an influence even on the Eddas. In one tale, Odin, the most powerful of the gods and the principal divinity of the Teutonic peoples, sacrifices himself by wounding himself with a spear and hanging himself from the axis of the world, the great ash tree Yggdrasil. A few days later, he is resurrected. This tale resonates quite powerfully with the story of the crucifixion in Christianity, although there is some debate as to whether this similarity is real or merely coincidental.

According to Scandinavian mythology, at the dawn of time

there was nothing but a vast, empty abyss. The first material to form was a realm of clouds and shadows called Niflheim, which appeared in the north of the abyss. Within the drifting mists of Niflheim appeared a fountain, Hvergelmir, from which twelve icy rivers sprang. In the south there emerged a realm of fire called Muspellsheim, which released its own rivers. However, the water in these rivers contained a powerful poison that gradually set into a solid mass. When the icy waters from the north touched this mass, the result was a huge deposit of hoarfrost that partly filled the primeval abyss. The frost eventually began to melt due to the warm air flowing from Muspellsheim, and from these water drops was formed the first living being, a giant named Ymir.

Ymir fell asleep and was covered with sweat, and under his left arm were born two more giants, a man and a woman. These offspring were wet-nursed by a cow, Audumla, which also came forth from the meltwater. While Ymir quenched his thirst at her great udder, Audumla licked the blocks of ice and took sustenance from the salt they contained. As she licked the ice away, she revealed, little by little, another being, called Buri. Buri had a son, Bor, who married a giantess named Bestla. Their three offspring were the gods Odin, Vili, and Ve.

Immediately the three gods turned on the giants, first killing Ymir. So vast was the torrent of blood that burst from his body that the primeval abyss was filled with it, and all the other giants were drowned, except for Bergelmir, who escaped with his wife in a small boat. These last surviving giants were the progenitors of a new race.

The three gods Odin, Vili, and Ve then raised Ymir's body from the waves, and with it formed the earth. It was situated halfway between Niflheim and Muspellsheim, and so they called it Midgard, the "middle abode." The dead giant's flesh became the land, and his blood became the sea; from his bones mountains were fashioned, and his hair became the trees. Next, the gods took his skull, and from it fashioned the heavens, placing within it the myriad random sparks that had drifted from the fires of Muspellsheim. Two of these sparks became the sun and the moon; the rest became the stars.

Presently, the first three gods were joined by others (the Scandinavian authors do not say where they came from), and together they set to work constructing their abode, the celestial realm of Asgard, the "abode of the Aesir," in which each god had his palace. They then built a bridge out of a rainbow, Bifrost, to connect Asgard with the realm of humans.

Their work completed, the Aesir then assembled and discussed how best to populate the earth. They noticed that grubs had begun to grow in the rotting corpse of Ymir; from these grubs they made the dwarfs. Since the dwarfs had been born from the flesh of Ymir, which had now become the earth, the Aesir decided that the dwarfs should dwell within the earth. There were no women in the race of dwarfs, so their numbers were replenished by new dwarfs born from the body of the earth.

Human beings were born of the vegetable world. It is told that one day three gods — Odin, Hoenir, and Lodur — were traveling across the earth when they saw two lifeless trees. The gods decided to turn them into mortal beings, so Odin gave them breath, Hoenir gave them a soul and intelligence, and Lodur gave them warmth. When they had finished, the first man and woman stood before them. The man was called Ask (Ash), and the woman was called Embla (Vine).

The earth on which the first humans lived was seen as a vast, circular land completely surrounded by water. The ocean was itself circular, and was bounded on its outer edge by the primeval abyss. In the depths of the ocean lived the titanic world serpent, whose coils encircled the earth.

There was another world beneath Midgard, which the Scandinavians called Niflheim. It was the abode of the dead and was filled with cold, damp mists. Besides the souls of the dead, giants and dwarfs lived here. Niflheim was the realm of the goddess Hel, and its entrance was guarded by the terrifying demon dog Garm, who prevented the living from entering. Niflheim also is the name given in the earliest legends to the northern region of the primeval abyss from which the world emerged. A possible explanation for this apparent inconsistency is that the later Norse poets were influenced by Greek and Oriental legends, and restructured their universe in three layers: Asgard, the world of the gods; Midgard, the human world; and Niflheim, the subterranean realm of the dead.

Upon the axis of these three worlds stood the great ash tree Yggdrasil, with its roots in the subterranean realm of Niflheim and its boughs spread above Asgard. The ancient fountain Hvergelmir gushed forth near one of Yggdrasil's roots; while the fountain of Mimir, the source of all wisdom, flowed beside another root, which extended into the realm of the giants. It was from this fountain that Odin would later drink, even though the price was one of his eyes. Beneath the tree's third root flowed the fountain of Urd, the wisest member of a race called the Norns. The Norns drew water from their fountain every day and sprinkled it on the root to nourish and preserve Yggdrasil.

In the tree's highest branches lived a golden cock, which kept a lookout for the enemies of the gods and warned them whenever danger approached. Yggdrasil also contained the horn of Heimdall, upon which the god would later blow at the commencement of the final battle that would see the destruction of the gods and of the universe itself. Within its branches lived the goat Heidrun, whose milk the gods drank.

The enemies of the gods frequently attempted to destroy Yggdrasil. The monstrous serpent Nidhögg dwelled beneath its third root, constantly chewing at it in an attempt to undermine the ash tree, while four stags nibbled at the foliage, consuming the young buds as soon as they appeared. The Norns, however, never ceased to care for the tree, ensuring that it continued to grow and thrive.

The Allfather

Although the Vikings worshiped a large number of divinities, the three main gods in their pantheon were Odin, Thor, and Tyr. These and other gods belonged to a race called the Aesir. There was another race of gods called the Vanir, the best known of which was the god Frey, closely identified with his twin sister, Freyja. In the distant past, a terrible struggle took place between the Aesir and the Vanir, but the two races joined forces in their frequent wars against the giants.

Odin, known as the Allfather (and Woden by the Germanic tribes), was the chief god — the god of war, justice, death, and wisdom. He took the form of a handsome man who liked to express himself in verse, and also was a shape shifter who could appear in whatever form he wished. Dressed in a golden helmet and breastplate, Odin carried the spear Gungnir, which had been forged by the dwarfs and which no armor could deflect. His horse, Sleipnir, had eight hooves, and was faster than any other and capable of overcoming any obstacle. It was Odin who ordered that dead warriors be burned with all their belongings, so that they would find them again in the afterlife.

Odin held court in a gigantic hall called Valhalla, the Hall of the Slain, to which all warriors who had died in battle were sent. The walls were made of spears, and the roof of shields. It was lit by huge fires burning at the centers of the feasting tables, and was entered by 540 colossal doors, each wide enough to admit 800 men standing abreast. The fallen warriors would spend all day in friendly but bloody battle, their bodies magically restored to health in the evening, which would be spent laughing, drinking, and feasting. All this would be watched over by Odin himself. On his shoulders sat two crows called Hugin (Thought) and Munin (Memory), which he sent out into the worlds of the living and the dead to gather news for him.

With the chief of the gods lived supernatural women called

Valkyries. It was their job to serve the dead warriors who were the guests of Odin, replenishing their plates and drinking horns following the battles of the day. However, the Valkyries had other important duties: during a battle on earth, it was their job to move unseen among the combatants and decide which warriors should die and be given the honor of joining Odin in Valhalla. Dressed in breastplates and helmets and carrying spears of flashing steel, they made their presence known only to those who were about to fall, informing them of their fate and then returning to Valhalla to inform Odin of their decisions.

Odin was as great a lover as he was a warrior. He was the husband of the goddess Frigg, but they had a rather relaxed relationship, and each was unfaithful to the other. Odin often would pursue mortal women as well as female giants. He also was wise and often benevolent, and had a profound knowledge of the magic embodied in the runes, which he discovered and taught to men. He often appeared as a one-eyed man, a legend arising from Odin's insatiable thirst for knowledge. In his quest, he consulted his maternal uncle, Mimir, a water demon whose fountain of knowledge stood near the ash tree Yggdrasil. Odin asked his uncle if he might drink from this fountain; Mimir agreed only on the condition that Odin give him one of his eyes as a pledge. Later Mimir was killed in the war between the Aesir and the Vanir, but Odin preserved his head and, with the aid of certain magical formulas, maintained the life within it. In this way Odin was able to take advantage of his uncle's knowledge whenever he chose.

Odin owed his great skill in poetry to the hydromel, the mead of the poets, which he stole from the giants who owned it. The hydromel was created by the Aesir and the Vanir after they had made peace with each other. The two races took a vase, and each spat into it. From their saliva they fashioned a man they called Kvasir, who was the wisest of all men. Kvasir was killed by two dwarfs who mixed his blood with honey and kept the mixture, the hydromel, in the cauldron Odrerir, after which it was named. Whoever drank the hydromel received the gifts of poetry and wisdom.

The two dwarfs also killed the father of a giant named Suttung. When Suttung discovered their crime he demanded that they give him the hydromel, which he hid in a vast subterranean chamber guarded by his daughter Gunnlöd. Odin, having decided to take the hydromel for himself, befriended Suttung's brother Baugi, and persuaded him to drill a hole through the massive rocks covering the entrance to Suttung's cave. Odin then transformed himself into a snake and slithered through the narrow opening. Once inside the cave, Odin changed back into his own form (that of an incredibly handsome man) and introduced himself to Suttung and Gunnlöd under an assumed name. Presently he won Suttung's friendship and Gunnlöd's love. He spent three nights with Gunnlöd, and each night she allowed him to drink from the cauldron of hydromel. By the third night he had succeeded in emptying the cauldron, whereupon he transformed himself into an eagle and escaped from the enraged giants. Suttung also changed himself into an eagle and attempted to give chase, but he died in the attempt. When Odin reached Asgard, he spat out the hydromel into a number of vases, from which he allowed his favorite poets to drink.

Numerous stories describe the adventures and exploits of Odin the Allfather. One of these tells how he was in a restless mood one day, and stalked up and down the hall of Valhalla. To his wife, Frigg, he cried: "I have such a fever in my blood that I must leave to travel far and wide. I am minded to go and visit the wise giant Vafthrudnir."

Frigg regarded her husband with trepidation and replied: "I would much rather the Father of Hosts remained here in the abode of the gods; for I believe that Vafthrudnir has no equal when it comes to wisdom and power."

Odin was undeterred, reminding his wife that he had traveled far in his life and learned a great many things. He longed to know what the company was like in Vafthrudnir's high hall, and announced his intention to go and find out. Frigg sighed in resignation, but warned her husband that he was about to embark on a potentially perilous journey. "Journey safely!" she cried. "And return safely, and may your wisdom be sufficient when you meet the wise giant."

Odin left Asgard, traveling across the trembling rainbow that was the bridge, Bifrost, connecting Asgard with the worlds of men, dwarfs, and giants. He wore a wide-brimmed hat so no one might see that he had lost an eye and know his true identity, and strode across the landscape, past singing streams and hissing rivers; across snow-covered plains that spat out great jets of steam from far underground.

Eventually he reached the mouth of a great valley, surrounded by majestic mountains that pondered silently and eternally in their cloaks of purple. Nestled in the valley was the high hall of the wise giant Vafthrudnir. Without further ado, Odin strode into the hall and called out: "Greetings, Vafthrudnir! I have come to your hall to meet you in person, for I have heard much concerning your wisdom, and I am wondering if it is as great as people say!"

Vafthrudnir began to fume at this less than tactful declaration by the stranger. "Who are you?" he demanded angrily. "Do you think you can insult me in my own hall? May you not leave this place alive unless you turn out to be the wiser one."

"I am called Gagnrad," declared Odin. "I have journeyed long to reach your hall, giant, and I am thirsty and in need of hospitality. Will you not offer me a little warmer welcome than this?"

With an apparent softening of his mood, Vafthrudnir beckoned to Odin, saying, "Why do you speak from the floor? Come and take a seat in the hall. Make yourself at home, and then we shall test which one knows more, the guest or the old sage."

"The poor man who comes to the wealthy one should keep to the point or say nothing," declared Odin, taking the offered seat. "To be too talkative brings bad results."

"Very well," said the giant. "Tell me, if you fancy your luck, what is the name of the stallion that draws the Day to mankind?"

Odin replied: "That horse is called Skinfaxi — Shining Mane — the very best of horses, whose mane shines with fire."

The giant then said: "Tell me then, if you fancy your luck, what is the name of the stallion that draws Night from the east to the beneficent gods?"

Odin replied: "That horse is called Hrimfaxi — Frost Mane — and from his bit foam falls every morning, and that is the source of the dew in the valleys."

Vafthrudnir then said: "Tell me then, if you fancy your luck, what is the name of the river that divides the earth between the sons of giants of the gods?"

Odin replied: "That river is called Ifing, and it will flow freely through all time, for ice will never form upon it."

The giant said: Very well; tell me then, if you fancy your luck, what is the plain called upon which Surt and the sweet gods will meet and do battle?"

Odin answered: "That plain is named Vigrid, and Surt and the sweet gods will meet and fight there; and one hundred leagues it stretches in each direction."

This first bout of questioning over, the wise giant sat back and reflected for a few moments. Presently he said: "You know a great deal, guest, about a great many things. Come, sit with me here on the giant's bench, and we shall speak further. We shall wager our heads on our wisdom: the loser in our contest shall forfeit his life!"

"Agreed!" cried Odin, and began to ask Vafthrudnir questions. "Tell me, giant, if your knowledge is sufficient, where did the earth and sky come from at the beginning of time?"

Came the reply: "The earth was shaped from Ymir's flesh, and the mountains from his bones. From his skull was the sky fashioned, and the sea from his blood."

"Tell me this second thing, if your knowledge is sufficient," said Odin. "Where did the sun and moon come from to travel over the world of men?"

Came the reply: "The sun and moon are the offspring of Mundilfæri, and they must journey through the sky every day, to mark the passage of time for men."

"Tell me this third thing, if your wisdom is sufficient," said Odin. "Where does Day come from, or Night with its new moons?"

The giant replied: "Delling is the father of Day, and Night is the offspring of Norr. The moon in its brightness and darkness were made by the beneficent Powers to count the years for men."

"Tell me this fourth thing, if you are really so wise," said Odin. "From where did the freezing winter and warm summer come from to the wise gods?"

Vafthrudnir replied: "He is called Vindsval — Wind Cold — the father of winter, and Svosud — the Mild One — sired the gentle summer."

"Tell me this fifth thing, if you believe you know the answer," said Odin. "Who was the eldest of the giants, and who were his offspring?"

The wise giant replied: "Uncounted winters before the earth was made, Bergelmir was born; Thrudgelmir was his father, and Aurgelmir was his grandfather."

"Tell me this sixth thing, if your knowledge is sufficient," said Odin. "Where did Aurgelmir come from in the dim and distant past?"

Vafthrudnir replied: "Drops of poison sprang forth from Elivagar, and they grew until out of them arose a giant. Thus began the race of giants, and thus they are all terrifying."

"Tell me this seventh thing, since you are said to be wise," said Odin. "How did that giant produce offspring, when he sported with no giantesses?"

Vafthrudnir replied: "It is said that underneath the giant's armpits a boy and girl grew together, and with one leg and the other leg that giant bore a son with six heads."

"Tell me this eighth thing, if you are so wise," said Odin. "What is your own first memory, you wisest of giants, who knows all things?"

The giant replied: "Bergelmir was born uncounted winters before the creation of the world, and my own first memory is of that mighty giant being laid in the gently rocking boat that was his coffin."

"Tell me this ninth thing, wise Vafthrudnir," said Odin. "Where does the wind come from, that travels over the waves and yet is never seen by men?"

Vafthrudnir replied: "The wind is caused by the flapping of the great wings of the eagle Hræsvelg — the Swallower of Corpses — who sits at the end of the world."

"Tell me this tenth thing, wisest of giants," said Odin. "Since you know of the fates of all the gods, from where did Njord come to the Aesir? For he rules over many temples and sanctuaries, although he was neither begotten nor raised by the Aesir."

The wise giant replied: "Njord was created by the Vanir in Vanaheim; and when doom finds the gods at the end of the world, he shall rejoin his wise people."

"Tell me this eleventh thing, if your knowledge is sufficient," said Odin. "Who are the men who fight every day in Odin's hall?"

Vafthrudnir replied: "They are heroes who have fallen in battle while on earth. Now they do battle with each other again, every day; and at the end of each day they are restored to health, and sit down to feast with each other."

"Tell me this twelfth thing, if you are wise enough," said Odin. "How do you know so much about the history and fate of all the gods?"

The giant replied: "I am able to read the runes of the gods and the runes of the giants; and I have traveled through every world, and even through Niflheim, the mist-shrouded world of the dead."

Said Odin: "I, too, have traveled far and learned many things, but tell me this: Who will survive when the Mighty Winter comes upon men?"

The giant replied: "Lif and Lifthrasir will hide in Hoddmimir's Wood; they will have the morning dew for food; and from them, new generations will spring."

"Much have I learned from my many travels," continued Odin. "Can you tell me from where the sun will return after the mighty wolf, Fenrir, has torn her apart?"

Came the reply: "Alfrothul — the Elf Disc — will bear a daughter before Fenrir attacks her; and her daughter shall walk in her paths when doom has found the gods."

"I know much of the ways and fates of the gods," continued Odin. "But tell me this: Who are those wise maidens who journey over the sea?"

Vafthrudnir replied: "They are of the race of Mogthrasir; they travel over settlements, and bring luck to the world; they possess the blood of giants, and they are protectors of men."

"Then answer me this," said Odin. "Who shall rule over the world of the gods when Surt's fire has been extinguished?"

"Vidar and Vali will live in the temples of the gods when Surt's fire has been slaked. Modi the Wrathful and Magni the Mighty will own the hammer Mjollnir for battle strength."

"And how, wise giant, will Odin's life end when the final doom is upon the gods and they are destroyed?"

The giant replied: "The wolf Fenrir will swallow the Allfather. His death will be avenged by Vidar, who will seize Fenrir and rip his mighty jaws asunder."

Leaning forward, Odin uttered his final question: "Tell me, wise Vafthrudnir, what words did Odin the Allfather whisper into the ear of his son Balder before the flames of the pyre consumed him?"

The wise giant regarded his guest carefully, and presently came to realize his true identity. "No one knows what you said in bygone days into your son's ear. I have been speaking my wisdom with a doomed mouth, for I have been contending in wisdom with Odin himself, who will always be the very wisest of beings."

Another story relates how King Hraudung of the Goths had two sons: Agnar, who was ten years old, and Geirrod, who was eight. One day, the boys decided to go fishing, so they gathered together their tackle and took their little boat out onto the sea. Soon, however, the wind rose and took hold of the boys' boat, casting it so far out onto the ocean that they soon lost sight of land. The light faded as night drew in upon them, bathing them in cold darkness as they sat helplessly in their tiny vessel. The sea took hold of them, tossing them on its surface like a discarded toy, and finally it dashed them on the treacherous rocks on the shoreline, leaving their boat a splintered wreck. Agnar and Geirrod stood — shaken, cold, and soaked through — while the sea thrashed mockingly around them. They looked at each other and realized, with lead in their hearts, that they were completely and hopelessly lost.

When dawn broke the following day, the young brothers left the sea's edge and came upon a poor farmer. When they told him their sorry tale, the good peasant invited them to spend the winter with him and his wife. The boys were well looked after: while the old woman took care of Agnar, her husband took charge of Geirrod, going on long walks along the shore with him, during which he taught him many things. Such was the old farmer's generosity that when spring came, he gave to the boys the boat he had built that winter.

When it was time for the boys to leave, they all walked down to the shore, whereupon the farmer spoke privately to Geirrod for a few moments. Then the lads stepped aboard their new boat, and the breeze took them out onto the water. Eventually they reached their father's harbor.

Geirrod was forward in the prow of the boat and jumped ashore. But before his elder brother could join him, he shoved the boat off again, shouting: "Go where the trolls will take you!" The boat drifted out to sea again, with Agnar still on board.

When he entered his father's hall, Geirrod was greeted joyfully by the people, who were surprised to see him still alive and who begged him to tell them of his adventures these past few months. Geirrod told them what had happened, adding

the dreadful lie that his elder brother had been lost overboard weeks previously and drowned. The people were
greatly saddened, and responded with their own lamentable
news that King Hraudung had died during Geirrod's absence. With the heir to the throne also dead, Geirrod was
crowned king of the Goths. Although great things were expected of Geirrod, he did not live up to the people's hopes:
he proved himself a cruel and tyrannical ruler, and became
notorious throughout the lands of the North.

In truth, the farmer and his wife were none other than
Odin and Frigg in disguise. Now the god and goddess sat on
their high seats and looked down on the world of Midgard.
"Look at Agnar, your foster son," said Odin disdainfully. "He
is living with a giantess in a cave and raising children with
her. Look at them! What brutish offspring! But Geirrod, my
foster son, is a great and strong king."

"But he is also a brute," retorted Frigg. "He is cruel, and
is such a miser that he tortures his dinner guests if it seems to
him that too many have come!"

"That is a lie," muttered Odin, and the two of them argued a little more until they decided to settle the matter one
way or the other. Frigg sent her maidservant, Fulla, to Geirrod
with a message.

"Beware," said Fulla to the king, "of a wizard who has
come to your country and intends to bewitch you. You will
know him by this sign: not even the fiercest dog is brave
enough to attack him."

It so happened that Frigg had indeed slandered Geirrod
when she said he was stingy with his food. In spite of his violent rage and casual cruelty, he was generous with all his
guests. He took heed of Fulla's warning, and presently had
his henchmen arrest a traveler whom no dog would attack.
The traveler was hauled before Geirrod in his hall. The traveler wore a blue cloak and called himself Grimnir. When he
was asked where he came from, the stranger refused to answer, and this made Geirrod yet more suspicious of him.
Certain that he had some dark and dangerous secret to hide,

the king ordered that Grimnir be tied up and placed before two roaring fires. This torture, surely, would be sufficient to loosen the traveler's tongue. Grimnir was left between the two fires for eight nights but kept his silence.

King Geirrod had a son who was ten years old and who was named Agnar, after Geirrod's brother. He was a sweet child, whom everyone at court loved dearly. When he saw how Grimnir suffered between the fires, he took him a horn to drink from, saying that the king was wrong to torture an innocent man.

Grimnir gratefully accepted the horn. The flames had by this time come so close that his cloak began to burn. Then Grimnir began to speak at great length, and said: "Fire, you are too hot and fierce. My cloak is burning. I have been here for eight nights, and my sufferings have been ignored by all except Agnar, and he alone shall rule over the land of the Goths.

"Blessed be you, Agnar! Odin bids you be blessed, and you shall never be better rewarded for the gift of a drink.

"Listen to me, while I tell you that the land where the gods live is sacred, and Thor will live in Thrudheim until the gods are torn asunder. The other gods have their own halls: the first is called Yewdale, and is occupied by Ull; the second is called Aflheim, and was given to Freyr when he cut his first tooth. The third is called Valaskjalf, the Hall of the Slain, which is thatched with silver. The fourth is called Sokkvabekk, and cool waves resound over it, and every day Odin and Saga drink joyfully from golden goblets.

"The fifth hall is called Gladsheim, the home of gladness, and nearby stands Valhalla, where dead heroes battle each other. The roof of the hall is made of shields, and its rafters are spears; mail-coats litter the benches, a wolf stands at the western door, while an eagle hovers above.

"The sixth hall is called Thrymheim, a violent place in the mountains, once inhabited by the terrible giant Thiazi, but now home to his beautiful daughter, Skadi. Breidablik is the name of the seventh hall; its name means Broad Splendor, and it stands in a very beautiful country where there is no evil. It is the home of Balder.

"The eighth hall is called Himinbjorg — the Cliffs of Heaven — where Heimdall lives, drinking god mead while he watches over the other gods. The ninth hall is called Folkvang, the Field of Folk, where dwells the goddess Freyja, who shares the slain with Odin.

"Glitnir is the tenth hall; it has golden buttresses and its roof is made of silver. Forseti lives there, and settles all disputes among the gods. The eleventh is Noatun, and belongs to Njord the blameless, who rules over a high-timbered temple. The twelfth is called Vidi, and there Vidar lives in a land of tall brushwood. Every day, the gods meet and hold council at the Well of Urd, Thor having waded across the Kormt and Ormt Rivers, while the other gods ride across the bridge Bifrost."

Finally the stranger concluded his speech thus: "Now I will tell you my names. I am called Mask, I am called Wanderer, Warrior and Helmet Wearer, the Pleasant One and the Third; I am Thud and Ud, Hell Blind and High One; I am Sad and Svipal and Sanngetal, War-merry, Flame-eyed, Bolverk, Fjolnir, the Hooded One, Maddener, and Much-wise; Broadhat, Broadbeard, War-father, Father of All, Father of the Slain, and Burden-god. I have never been known by just one name since I came upon humans in Midgard.

"Here in Geirrod's hall I am called Grimnir. When I traveled upon a sledge I was called Keel Ruler, and at the gods' Assembly I am known as Thror. In battle I am called Vidur, and the gods also call me Spear-shaker, Fulfiller of Desire and Wand-bearer."

With that, the stranger turned his furious and terrifying gaze on King Geirrod, who, along with his retainers, had been fast asleep in the great hall the whole time. "Drunk you are, Geirrod," he growled. "You have drunk too much, and you lose much when you lose my favor. The gods are now against you; your life is over; we have nothing but death to offer you. Look at me, for I am now called Odin!"

Geirrod sat listening to this, with his sword half drawn from its sheath. When he heard the stranger reveal that he was Odin, the king sprang up with the intention of freeing him from the fires. But as he lurched forward, he stumbled, and his sword fell from its sheath and hit the floor hilt first. Geirrod fell on it, was impaled, and died there and then.

At that point, Odin vanished. Agnar became king, and ruled for a long time.

One of the most fascinating of the myths associated with Odin is his voluntary self-sacrifice on the mighty world tree Yggdrasil. Wounded by his own spear consecrated to himself, he hung from the tree for nine days and nights, buffeted by the winds howling through its great branches. This sacrifice and the resurrection that followed it were magical acts of self-rejuvenation, for the Norse gods grew old just as did humans. While hanging from the tree, Odin looked down and perceived some runes, which he managed to lift into the air. Their magic power set him free, and he dropped to the ground, his youth, strength, and vitality fully restored. Mimir then gave him some hydromel, restoring his wisdom and skill in poetry. While it is possible that this legend was inspired by Christ's suffering on the cross, historians maintain that it has more in common with the shamanic rituals of central Asia, in which the shaman must undergo certain trials in the spirit world, where his body is destroyed and remade. We also must remember that Odin was not considered immortal: he was ultimately doomed to die and disappear forever from the world.

God of Thunder

Thor, who was called Donar by the German tribes, was comparable to Odin in power and importance; some of the

Teutonic tribes even considered him to be the first and most powerful of all the gods. As such, he was greatly feared by the tribes, who felt his presence keenly whenever they heard the terrifying crash of thunder. They believed that the sound was that of Thor's chariot wheels as he rode across the gray, ironclad heavens. When lightning struck, it was Thor's weapon descending on the earth. The Germanic tribes believed it to be an ax, while the Norse people believed it was a great stone hammer.

To the Vikings, Thor was the quintessential warrior. Immensely strong, he possessed nobility and brutality in equal measure. He knew neither fear, nor the need to rest from his frequent battles with giants, demons, and all manner of other monsters. If Odin was the god of warriors who fell in battle, poets, and the wise, Thor was the god of rough peasants, utterly lacking in subtlety and eloquence. Thor knew neither fear nor the ignominy of defeat. His beard was long and red, and his voice so loud that it easily carried above the chaotic noise of battle. It was the voice of Thor that inspired the Teutonic tribes to shout at the tops of their lungs when attacking their enemies.

The weapon with which Thor is most closely associated is, of course, the mighty war hammer. Some legends say that it fell as a meteorite from the sky, accompanied by a thunderbolt, while others maintain that it was the handiwork of a dwarf. It was indeed a powerful and terrible weapon: when Thor threw it, the hammer would find its target without fail, and would then fly back to the hand of its master. If Thor needed to conceal it, it would shrink until it was small enough for him to slip it into his clothing. The hammer's name was Mjölnir (Destroyer), and so great was its power that Thor needed a pair of magical iron gloves with which to grasp it. He also possessed a girdle that doubled his strength.

Thor lived in Asgard with the other gods of the Norse pantheon. His palace, the largest in Asgard, was called Bilskirnir, and stood in the region of Thrudvang (Field of Strength). His great passion was to strike out from his palace and roam far and wide throughout the world in his chariot, which was drawn by two he-goats. When he became hungry, Thor would kill the goats and cook them. This was no loss to him, however, for the next day he would place his hammer on their hides, and they would reappear with all their previous strength and desire to serve. Thor's mother was the goddess Jörd. His wife, Sif, was said to be the epitome of faithfulness. He had two sons, Magni (Strength) and Modi (Anger), who, it was believed, would one day inherit his hammer and replace him when the world was remade.

While immensely brave and skilled in battle, Thor was not blessed with the sharpest of intellects, and sometimes he would be tricked by monsters and demons, although he would invariably vanquish them in a physical confrontation. One such adventure began when Thor awoke one morning to find his hammer missing. He sought the aid of the cunning trickster god Loki (whom we shall meet again later). Loki suggested that the hammer had been stolen by a giant, and offered his services in retrieving it. He went to the goddess Freyja and borrowed a robe of feathers that gave the power of flight to the wearer; then he flew to the realm of the giants, where he encountered a giant named Thrym. The giant confessed to stealing Thor's hammer, but refused to return it unless he was given Freyja as a wife. Loki returned to the Aesir with Thrym's demand. At first outraged and incredulous, the gods held a meeting and reluctantly decided that there was nothing to do but ask Freyja to give herself to Thrym. The goddess immediately flew into a rage and absolutely refused. A little shamefacedly, the other gods returned to their deliberations and presently hit on a plan to retrieve Thor's hammer. When he heard the plan, the thunder god was unimpressed, to say the least, since it involved his dressing in a bridal veil and pretending to be Freyja.

Presently Thor agreed to the scheme, and went to the realm of the giants with Loki, who pretended to be a servant. At Thrym's palace, the two Aesir were given a lavish welcome as the giant gave orders for the wedding banquet to begin immediately. Although he was impersonating Freyja, Thor ate very much with his own appetite, and consumed an enormous amount, including a whole ox, eight large salmon, and three barrels of mead. Thrym was nonplussed, but Loki quickly stepped in and explained that "Freyja" had been so excited about her approaching wedding that she had been unable to eat for more than a week.

Thrym was deeply impressed, and his love (not to mention his lust) grew in leaps and bounds. Unable to contain himself, he lifted "Freyja's" veil to steal a kiss . . . and was greeted with a pair of terrifying eyes that flashed lightning, forcing him to jump back. Once again, Loki offered an explanation: it was the fever of love and passion, he said, that caused those eyes to flash so brightly.

Thrym could wait no longer for the "goddess" to be his, and ordered his servants to bring forth the hammer, Mjölnir. In addition to being a weapon of war, Thor's hammer was used to consecrate marriage contracts. The giant placed the weapon on "Freyja's" knees, according to the custom, whereupon Thor stood up and, throwing off his veil, attacked Thrym and all the other giants in the palace, felling them with ease. His prize possession successfully retrieved and the thief punished, Thor returned with Loki to Asgard.

Many monsters as well as giants fell before the might of Thor's hammer. On one occasion he decided to kill the world serpent of Midgard, which caused the violent storms in the vast ocean surrounding the earth. During his travels he met a giant named Hymir, who gave him shelter. When Hymir informed Thor that he was going fishing, Thor asked if he might come and help him. Thor was very young at that time, and the giant dismissed his offer with contempt, saying that he had no need of help from a lad such as he. Restraining his urge to beat the giant to a pulp then and there, Thor asked what bait he would be using. When Hymir replied that if he did not know, there was no point in telling him, Thor took hold of one of Hymir's bulls, ripped its head off, and threw it into the boat. This seemed to convince the giant that Thor was one to be reckoned with, so he allowed the lad to accompany him on the fishing trip. Out into the ocean they went, with Thor taking the oars, until Hymir ordered him to stop, for here was the giant's favored fishing spot, and farther than this he was afraid to venture.

Thor ignored him, however, and continued rowing toward that part of the sea where the world serpent lived. He then buried his fishing hook in the bull's head and hurled it into the sea. The serpent lost no time in seizing the bloody bait, and as soon as the hook bit into its flesh, the monster began to thrash wildly in the ocean, throwing up great clouds of spray. So violent was the serpent's thrashing that the boards of the fishing boat gave way. Now standing on the sea bottom, Thor increased his grip on the fishing line and succeeded in hauling part of the serpent's body into the boat. The serpent opened its vast maw wide and spat venom at the fishermen, while Thor stood firm and returned its hideous gaze, with lightning flashing from his own eyes.

This spectacle was too much for Hymir. The giant lost his nerve and, lunging forward, cut the line just as Thor was about to bring his hammer down on the world serpent's head. The great beast slithered off the boat and into the sea, and was gone. So enraged was he at Hymir's cowardice that Thor immediately turned and struck him savagely on the head with his hammer, sending the giant tumbling into the sea, where he drowned. Thor then walked back along the seabed to the shore.

These are only two of Thor's many exploits. Although he was far from the most intelligent or cultured of the gods, such were his strength and bravery that he was among the best loved in the entire Teutonic pantheon.

The Sky God

Although he plays only a small part in Germanic mythology, the sky god Tiw is spoken of often in the legends of the Far

North, where he is called Tyr. Some legends claim he was the son of the giant Hymir, while others claim that he was Odin's son. Extremely brave and clever on the field of battle, Tyr often decided which side would prevail in combat, so it was considered wise to invoke him before meeting one's enemies.

In one legend, an oracle warned the gods of the Aesir that the giant wolf Fenrir could do them considerable harm, and advised them to reduce the beast to a state in which he would be more manageable. They decided against killing him; instead, they would chain him up, but the chains they forged were useless against Fenrir's immense strength. The gods then consulted the dwarfs, and asked them to produce a chain that the wolf would be unable to break.

The dwarfs agreed, and soon presented the gods with a magical chain composed of six ingredients: the meow of a cat, the beard of a woman, the roots of a mountain, the tendons of a bear, the breath of a fish, and the spittle of a bird. Although the chain was soft as silk, it was tougher than any metal the gods had been able to fashion, and defied all their attempts to break it. Satisfied, they went to see Fenrir, and presented him with a challenge. The material, they said, was unbreakable; all of them had tried and failed. Perhaps Fenrir would care to demonstrate his own strength by breaking the chain?

Fenrir, however, suspected that the gods were up to something. But since he did not want to appear cowardly, he accepted the challenge on one condition: that one of the gods must place his hand in Fenrir's mouth. If the challenge turned out to be a trick, the wolf would bite off the hand. The gods exchanged glances; none was willing to put a hand between Fenrir's jaws, for they knew full well what would happen when the wolf found himself trapped by the magical chain.

Then Tyr stepped forward, and without a word placed his right hand in Fenrir's mouth. The rest of the Aesir then bound Fenrir in the chain, and as the wolf struggled to break free, the chain grew tighter and tighter until he was exhausted. When they saw that their plan had succeeded, the Aesir laughed. Tyr, however, did not, for he knew what was about to happen. When he realized that he had been tricked, Fenrir closed his mighty jaws on Tyr's hand, severing it at the wrist.

The Trickster

Loki is the enfant terrible of Scandinavian mythology. Although originally regarded as completely benevolent, he was represented more and more as mischievous, a subversive element who could at times be downright wicked. We have already seen how Loki helped Thor retrieve his hammer from the Giant thrym; but Loki seems to have been happiest when he was devising some trickery to undermine the power of the Aesir. His adventures are preserved in the Scandinavian skaldic poetry of the ninth and tenth centuries.

Originally a fire demon, Loki was the son of Farbauti, the origin of fire, and Laufey, the forested island who provided fuel for the fire. Loki's association with fire is remembered even today: in Norway, for example, it is said that the crackling of a fire is the sound of Loki thrashing his children. At the beginning of time, Loki and Odin swore eternal friendship and became blood brothers. Loki was very handsome and was extremely fond of consorting with the female gods, who all adored him. There was something diabolic in his charm, however, and with the spread of Christianity in Scandinavia he began to take on some of the attributes of the devil.

In the early days of the settlement of the gods, soon after they had established their presence in Midgard and had built Valhalla, the colossal Hall of the Slain, they looked at their abode of Asgard and decided that an impregnable wall should be built around it so they would be safe from the attentions of their enemies. The job would have to be done, they decided, but no one was particularly anxious to take on the burden himself. The gods passed some considerable time in fruitless debate as to how and by whom the great undertaking should be started.

One day, a solitary figure on horseback appeared, and was about to cross the bridge Bifrost when he was stopped by Heimdall the watchman, who asked him what his business was.

"I wish to put a proposition to the gods of Asgard," the stranger said.

Conscientious as ever, Heimdall stood his ground, saying: "There's no need to enter Asgard yourself: tell me your proposition, and I will see to it that the gods are made aware of it."

This was not satisfactory to the visitor, who replied: "I have no doubt they will be most interested in what I have to suggest, so it's only fair that I be allowed to speak to them in person. If you disagree, then I shall tell no one."

Heimdall thought for a moment, and then, grudgingly, allowed the traveler to cross Bifrost and approach Asgard.

The gods and goddesses gathered together and allowed the mysterious traveler to come before them. Dismounting from his impressive stallion, he strode to the center of the great hall and looked up into the faces of Odin and the twelve chief gods who were seated in their high places. All around milled lesser gods and the goddesses, all eager to hear what this audacious stranger thought so important that it demanded their attention.

Odin cast his piercing glance at the visitor and said: "Heimdall has asked us to gather here so that we might hear your words. What is it you wish to say?"

The stranger replied: "I have come to offer to build a wall around Asgard. It will stand tall and firm, and will turn back all who might wish to enter your realm without your permission. The stone giants will not be able to penetrate it, and neither will the frost giants, nor indeed any whom you would call enemies."

Odin nodded, and regarded the visitor through narrowed eyes. The chief of the gods was no fool, and strongly suspected that this monumental task would not be accomplished free of charge. "What are your conditions?" he asked slowly.

"I shall require eighteen months from the day I begin to the day I finish," came the reply.

"That seems well within the bounds of possibility," said Odin. "And what shall be your fee for the job?"

Without hesitation the stranger replied: "I want Freyja as my wife."

At this the entire hall erupted in a cacophony of howled protest, the gods stamping their feet and waving their fists at the impudent stranger, shouting that he be thrown out immediately.

Barely concealing his own rage, Odin declared that the stranger's price was too high, and so he might as well take himself off that very moment and not bother the gods of Asgard again. But instead of leaving the hall (and being thankful that he was still alive), the stranger remained where he was and added: "I not only wish for Freyja's hand, but also for the sun and the moon as payment."

This prompted a new round of shouting and insult-hurling, which died down at the sound of Loki's voice. "Surely we are being a bit hasty," he said smoothly. "There's no need to dismiss our visitor's request without giving it the slightest thought. We should consider it."

The other gods now fell completely silent, for they knew Loki well, and suspected that his sly mind was hatching some strange plan. Odin asked the visitor to leave them for a while, until they had had a chance to discuss his offer. Freyja, the exquisitely beautiful goddess whose hand the stranger had demanded as part of his payment, was sitting silently. She had not uttered a word since the stranger's arrival. Now, when she saw that the gods were about to give serious thought to the idea, she began to weep, and from her eyes flowed a steady stream of golden tears.

Now Loki addressed his fellows, saying: "Let's agree to what this man suggests . . . but give him *six* months to complete the task instead of eighteen. He'll never be able to do it in that time — he won't stand a chance. He'll be lucky to get half of the wall built, and even if he does, why, that's half a wall that *we* don't have to break our backs building!"

The gods considered this, and concluded that Loki's scheme could not fail: the builder would be given six months to complete his task, and if by the end of that time a single stone of the wall had yet to be laid, the agreement would be annulled and he would forfeit his payment.

When the builder had been readmitted to the hall of the gods, Odin called out to him: "We'll give you six months to build the wall. If you manage it, you shall have Freyja's hand in addition to the sun and the moon."

"Six months!" laughed the visitor. "There's no possibility of completing the wall in that time."

Odin continued regardless: "Tomorrow is the first day of winter. If you have not completed the wall by the first day of summer, you forfeit your payment. And you must do the job alone," he added. "No one shall help you in any way."

"Impossible!" declared the visitor. But then his eyes fell on Freyja, and his heart swelled with longing for the beautiful goddess. Turning again to Odin, he said: "I will build the wall in six months, as you ask, but to do so I will need the help of my stallion, Svadilfari. At least allow me that."

Odin declined this request, reiterating the gods' terms, to which the visitor replied that he would not undertake the wall's construction unless he was allowed the help of his horse. Growing exasperated, Loki cried: "Let him use his horse! He'll still never complete the job on time!"

The bargain was struck, and witnessed by all present, and was confirmed with many solemn oaths, since the builder did not consider it safe to be among the Aesir without safe conduct. He feared that he might have trouble with Thor (who was away in the East, fighting trolls) should the thunder god return home.

Well before sunrise on the following morning, the builder began his gargantuan task of building a wall around Asgard. He led his stallion Svadilfari to a hill whose flanks were exposed, revealing enormous masses of rock and boulders. The builder unfolded a vast net, which he harnessed to Svadilfari and filled with boulders. Presently he filled the net and called to his stallion to pull with all his might. The great animal's muscles strained and bulged, and he dragged the titanic mound of rock up the slope toward Asgard. By the time the sun appeared over the horizon, the builder and his horse had brought forth a veritable mountain of boulders with which to begin the task.

The gods and goddesses of Asgard awoke and looked out of their windows to see how the visitor was getting along. They were most surprised and more than a little irritated to see how much material he had already amassed. The Aesir watched in growing trepidation as the builder smashed the massive rocks into more manageable pieces, which he laid with great speed and consummate skill while his stallion rested nearby.

Throughout the winter, through rain, hail, snow, and biting winds, the stranger stuck to his task, never tiring, never ceasing his labors. As he continued, the Aesir began to wonder whether there might be more to this stranger than met the eye. Could he actually be a giant in disguise? It seemed more than likely, such was the strength and speed with which both he and his horse went back and forth between the hillside with its masses of exposed rock, and the swiftly growing wall around Asgard.

Three days before the end of spring, the wall stood all but complete; all that remained to be constructed was the gateway. The edifice was vast and high and magnificently built. It would, without a doubt, be sturdy enough to repel the attacks of all enemies.

Odin called a meeting of the gods while Freyja sat sobbing uncontrollably, covering the floor with her abject tears of glittering gold. She could not stop herself, for well she knew the fate that now almost certainly awaited her.

As silence fell in the hall, Odin addressed the assembly. "This is unacceptable!" he roared. "The mason is nearing the completion of his task, and on time! How did this happen?

How did we allow ourselves to enter into this agreement with its appalling price? When he leaves, he will take with him not only Freyja, but the sun and the moon as payment, and we shall be left to stumble around in impenetrable darkness and numbing cold for the rest of our lives. Whose idea was this? Who persuaded us to risk so much?"

All eyes fell on Loki. Odin stalked across the hall and stood before the trickster. As Odin grabbed him by the shoulders and started to squeeze, Loki looked at the others in desperation and cried: "But we all agreed — all of us! How was I to know he'd do so well? How were any of us to know?"

"You were the one who persuaded us to allow him the use of his horse!" thundered the chief of the gods. "It's your fault, and you must make it right. Think of a way to get us out of this agreement, and think fast, for if you fail, your life will be added to the account." As he made this threat, Odin squeezed tighter on Loki's shoulders, and the trickster began to feel his bones and tendons crunch.

"Very well!" he screamed. "I'll think of something. I'll get us out of this. I'll see that the builder goes away empty-handed. . . ."

That evening, the builder looked on his work with the greatest satisfaction. Soon, he told himself, the exquisite Freyja would be his, as would the sun and the moon. Whistling a happy tune, he led Svadilfari for what he assumed would be the last time to the hillside from which he had plucked the mountain of stone.

As the man and his horse prepared to haul the final load of stone to the wall around Asgard, a young mare appeared from behind a thicket and whinnied to Svadilfari. The great stallion's attention was immediately aroused, as was his ardor, and he tried to make off in pursuit of the new arrival. The mason struggled to keep him at bay, pulling with all his might on Svadilfari's reins. But the great stallion's strength and desire were too great; he broke the reins and galloped off in pursuit of the mare.

The mason was furious, and yelled after Svadilfari to come

back. Time was marching on, and the last thing he needed was
to lose the means by which he had built the wall with such
speed. The truth was, even though he only had to build the
gateway to claim his payment, even that task would be beyond
him in the time allowed, should Svadilfari fail to return quickly.

Svadilfari did not return quickly; he was away all that
night, frolicking with the young mare, and leaving the mason to watch the approaching glow of dawn with as much
trepidation as the Aesir had felt while watching him at work.
As the first day of summer dawned, the mason realized that
he would have no choice but to attempt to build the gateway
using the few pathetic lumps of rock left over from his labors
of the previous day. They were not enough, of course, and as
summer began, the builder's work was unfinished.

When he realized that all was lost, the mason flew into a
terrifying rage. He cast aside his disguise and stood regarding the Aesir with molten hatred. And the Aesir saw that he
was indeed a giant, and decided that no reverence need be
shown for the oaths they had made. Without hesitation, they
called on Thor, who arrived without delay.

The thunder god strode up to the giant, took hold of his
mighty hammer Mjölnir, and paid the giant his wages. It was
not Freyja, and it was not the sun and moon; it was not even
the chance to return to the realm of the giants; it was a single blow that shivered his huge skull into a myriad of bloody
fragments and sent him hurtling into Niflheim, the be-
nighted realm of the dead.

The Aesir were well satisfied with the way the affair had
turned out; however, they did not realize that the affair had
not yet ended. Loki was missing, and remained so for several
months. When he eventually returned to Asgard, admiring
the splendid wall as he arrived, the other gods saw that he
had brought a colt with him.

Odin walked up to him and remarked on the beauty and
unusual nature of the colt, which had eight legs. "His name
is Sleipnir," said Loki proudly, "and he is my son." The colt
was the result of Loki's dalliance with the giant's horse,

Svadilfari, while he was in the guise of the young mare. When he saw how Odin admired the colt, Loki gave it to him, saying that he would take Odin anywhere he pleased, and would be able to outrun all other horses.

Odin was tremendously pleased with this marvelous gift, and welcomed Loki back to Asgard with the greatest enthusiasm.

On this occasion, Loki got off lightly: he managed to secure the building of Asgard's wall, and present Odin with one of his most prized possessions in the bargain. The trickster's antics frequently got him into very serious trouble, and when this happened he had little compunction in sacrificing his fellow Aesir to extricate himself. One day, he was out traveling with Odin and another god, named Hoenir. The three decided to stop for a rest, and to roast an ox for dinner. They were spied by an eagle, who was perched high in a tree and who cast a spell on the ox, preventing it from cooking. The eagle said it would lift the spell only if the gods allowed it to share their meal. They agreed, but were dismayed when the eagle immediately took the best cuts of meat. This audacity was too much for Loki, who struck the eagle with a rod. As soon as he did so, Loki found that he could not let go of the rod, which remained attached to the eagle. The bird then flew away, dragging Loki behind it.

When Loki begged the eagle to let him go, it changed into its true form: the giant Thiazi. Immensely pleased to have caught a god, Thiazi agreed to let him go on one condition: that Loki delivered to him the goddess Idun and her magical apples, which prevented the Aesir from growing old. The apples were obviously hugely important to the Aesir, and their loss would have been a catastrophe for the inhabitants of Asgard. Nevertheless, Loki did not hesitate to agree, and lured Idun into a forest that contained, he claimed, apples of even greater beauty than her own. As planned, Thiazi appeared, pounced on the goddess, and dragged her away.

With the loss of Idun and her apples, the Aesir began to grow old. In rage they demanded that Loki bring her back, threatening him with all manner of suffering if he did not comply. Among the punishments they had planned for him was the horrible and legendary "blood eagle," in which the victim's spine would be split with a battle-ax, and his rib cage splayed out like the wings of an eagle. Having no desire to experience such a punishment, Loki transformed himself into a hawk and flew to the realm of the giants, where he found Idun and changed her into a nut. He carried her back to Asgard, but was pursued by Thiazi in his eagle form. The other Aesir witnessed the pursuit, and built an enormous fire on the border of Asgard. As the eagle flew over the fire, its wings were burned and it fell to its death in the flames.

The legends regarding Loki frequently portray him as the instigator of problems, which he then must use his cunning to solve lest the other gods destroy him in their anger. On one occasion he made an enemy of Thor after cutting off the beautiful hair of the thunder god's wife, Sif. When he discovered this, Thor grabbed Loki and began to break his bones one by one. In desperation, Loki said that he would persuade the dwarfs to make tresses of gold for Sif, which would grow like natural hair. Placated, Thor released him, and Loki went to the forges of the dwarfs. They agreed to make the golden hair, and also promised to build a ship, *Skidbladnir,* which would take its crew to any desired destination, and the spear Gungnir. Both these items were to be presented as gifts to Odin.

However, Loki could not keep himself out of trouble, for he made a bet with a dwarf named Brökk that he and his brother Sindri, who was a talented craftsman, would not be able to make such treasures as the other dwarfs had made. Even more foolishly, Loki bet them his own head, and so, fearing that they would win, he transformed himself into a gadfly and began to pester and sting them to distract them from their work. His efforts were in vain, for the two dwarfs fashioned three wondrous items: the ring Draupnir, which made its owner rich; a golden boar for the god Frey; and Thor's hammer.

The Aesir were called to examine the items and were

mightily impressed, especially with the hammer. They concluded that Brökk and Sindri had won the bet, and Loki's head belonged to them. Loki presented himself to the dwarf brothers, but as they moved to seize him, he vanished, being as he was in possession of a pair of shoes that could transport the wearer away from any danger. Brökk immediately complained to Thor, who pursued and caught Loki, and returned him to the dwarfs.

Loki, however, had one last trick up his sleeve. He said to the dwarfs that they indeed had the right to take his head — but nothing had been said in the wager regarding his neck. They therefore had no right to touch any part of his neck when cleaving his head from his body. The dwarfs, who were nowhere near as quick-witted as the wily Loki, conceded that to take his head would be impossible. Nevertheless, they insisted that they should be allowed to sew Loki's lips together, to prevent him from misleading people. This they did with a stout cord; but once they had left, Loki simply ripped the cord from his lips, and continued with his mischievous adventures.

It was these adventures that eventually got him into trouble with all the gods. He was not above insulting them to their faces, as described in one of the poems of the *Eddas*. His reputation was such that when the giant Aegir invited the gods and goddesses to a great feast in his hall, Loki was the only god not invited. This did not stop him from throwing open the doors of Aegir's hall and insolently presenting himself at the banquet. The other guests were less than pleased to see him, and fell silent in their irritation. Undaunted, Loki declared that he was just a weary traveler in need of a drink and a rest; surely he would not be denied these simple things. However, Bragi, the god of poetry, maintained that Loki should be turned away as the villainous ne'er-do-well he undoubtedly was.

Loki made a direct plea to Odin, reminding him of their oath of eternal friendship. The others talked among themselves and presently decided that they should make a place for him at their table, according to custom. Taking his cup in his hand, Loki drank to the health of all the other gods, with the exception of Bragi, whom he had not forgiven for wanting to turn him away. Bragi decided to make peace, and apologized, offering Loki a horse, a sword, and some rings. This was not enough for Loki, who declared that Bragi was a coward who never followed his friends into battle. Before Bragi could respond, his wife, Idun, begged him to ignore the jibe.

This only served to make Loki more angry and insolent, and he proceeded to insult them all in turn, reminding them of every scandal that had ever besmirched their reputations. As if this were not insulting enough, Loki proceeded to relate how all the goddesses had been unfaithful to their husbands — many with Loki himself. He continued with a list of all the crimes he had happily committed against each of the gods; and their attempts to return his insults only spurred him on to utter more vitriolic pronouncements.

Finally Sif, the wife of Thor, who was the only god not present at the banquet, having been traveling in the East, came forward and begged Loki to stop. With savage delight Loki turned on her, describing how she, too, had happily given herself to him. No sooner had Loki uttered the name of the thunder god than a titanic rumbling shook the hall. The doors burst open, and Thor entered, fixing Loki with his terrifying gaze. Loki was unperturbed, however, and proceeded to hurl insults at Thor himself. Without a word, Thor raised his hammer, fully intending to demolish Loki with a single stroke. At this point the interloper stopped, thought better of his actions, and retreated to the doors. Turning to Aegir, he declared that this would be the last time the giant would be able to give a feast such as this, for soon all his possessions would be destroyed by fire. With that, he left the hall.

Although the gods could not know it at the time, Loki's prophecy would be proved accurate — not only for Aegir, but for the entire world as well.

It was due to the actions of Loki that gold sometimes was known as "otter payment" or "strife metal." One day, when the worst of winter was over, Odin, Loki, and Hoenir decided to set out from Asgard and continue their exploration of the world. Crossing Bifrost, they headed into Midgard and, having braved a sudden late snowstorm, followed the course of a river to a great waterfall at its head.

There they spied an otter, quietly minding its own business, basking on the riverbank and holding a salmon it had just caught. Loki immediately saw his opportunity, and picked up a fist-size rock, which he hurled at the inoffensive creature. The stone struck the otter on its head, killing it instantly. Loki grabbed the otter and the salmon and climbed back up the riverbank to his companions. "Look at this!" he cried. "We shall certainly eat well this evening!"

Odin and Hoenir agreed, and all were well satisfied with the day's events. They continued up the river valley until the light began to fade, and they realized it would be necessary to find lodgings for the night if they didn't want to sleep beneath a cold blanket of stars. Luck was still with them, however, for soon they spied smoke rising from the chimney of a farmhouse a little way off.

Odin knocked on the door, and when the farmer answered, the god gave him a friendly greeting and asked if they might stay the night. The farmer, whose name was Hreidmar, asked: "How many are you?"

"There are three of us," replied Odin. "We do not expect to lodge for free. We have enough provisions with us for everyone."

Hreidmar was unconvinced. "I have two sons, Fafnir and Regin; and two daughters, Lyngheid and Lofnheid. Will there be enough for them?"

"Of course!" cried Odin. "There will be enough for everyone."

Hreidmar reluctantly agreed to allow the three visitors to stay the night. Loki presented the farmer with the otter and salmon, saying: "Here's the food, got with just one stone!"

When the farmer saw the dead otter under Loki's arm, his expression grew hard and, without another word, he left the room and his unwanted and bemused guests. He found his sons in another room and said angrily to them: "I have evil news: your brother Otter is dead, killed by three travelers who now ask for a night's lodgings here!"

Fafnir and Regin stood up with rage leaping in their hearts. "Then our guests will not leave this house alive," they said, "for we will avenge our brother's death!"

Hreidmar nodded. "We are equally matched, three against three," he said. It so happened that Hreidmar was well versed in the ways of magic. "I shall put spells upon them to weaken and bind them."

The three men then returned to their guests and without warning leaped on them. Hreidmar's magic spells took effect, and soon the three gods lay bound helpless before them. In response to their outraged demands for an explanation, the farmer replied: "The otter you killed was my son, who took that form by day, and was the finest of fishermen. You have killed my son!"

"We did not know he was your son," said Odin. "If we had known, we would never have killed him."

"Nevertheless," replied Hreidmar, "my son is dead, and you are responsible."

Odin repeated that they did not intentionally take the life of the farmer's son, and added: "Before you kill us, you must at least give us the chance to pay you an adequate ransom for your son's life. Name your price: we will pay whatever you demand."

Hreidmar looked at his two sons and then replied: "Very well. Fafnir, Regin, find Lyngheid and Lofnheid, and have them flay Otter and bring his skin to me." When Otter had been flayed and his skin had been laid out beside the roaring fire, the farmer turned to the three gods and said: "This is the ransom: you must fill my son's skin with gold, and when his skin has been completely filled, you must then cover it with more gold until not one piece of it can be seen."

Odin agreed, and, turning to Loki, whispered in his ear. Loki nodded, and said to the farmer: "If you release me, I will go to fetch the gold. Keep my companions as hostages, and you may be sure that I will return."

Hreidmar agreed, and released Loki from his bonds, whereupon the god opened the door and disappeared into the night.

Although it was his intention to keep his word, Loki was in no great hurry to do so, and took his time crossing Midgard to the island of Hlesey. In the hall of Aegir and Ran he asked to borrow a net with which he might save the lives of his comrades. The sea god and goddess reluctantly agreed to lend him their net, and Loki left their hall and made for the realm of the dwarfs.

To reach his objective, Loki had to navigate a seemingly endless series of dank tunnels and dripping caves, a vast labyrinth carved inside the flesh of the world. Eventually he came to a gigantic cave that was dimly lit by a shaft connecting it with the world outside; and in a great pool at the center of this cavern he found what he was looking for. With his borrowed net, he caught a vicious-looking fish. Taking the creature in both hands, he shook it violently, commanding it to change shape. Eventually it did so, and became the dwarf Andvari.

"What do you want?" he demanded.

"Your gold," Loki replied laconically. "Or I'll kill you here and now."

Andvari was crestfallen, but he perceived that he had little choice but to give Loki what he demanded, so he led him from the vast cavern to his smithy. Loki looked around the hot, smoky chamber at the piles of gold that lay glittering in the firelight, and was well satisfied. Andvari gathered up all the gold and filled two large sacks with it, muttering under his breath as he did so. When the two sacks has been filled and placed before him, Loki said: "That's not all of it: you're hiding a ring from me." He pointed to the dwarf's right hand, which was gripping something.

Andvari shook his head. "No," he replied, "that's it; you've got the lot."

"Put the ring in the sack."

"No, let me keep it. Just the ring; you take everything else."

"I said put the ring in the sack!"

"Just let me keep this ring," Andvari pleaded. "With it, I'll be able to make more gold."

"I'm taking all the gold you have," insisted Loki. He stepped forward, seized Andvari's fist, and forced it open to reveal the beautifully crafted ring. So impressed was he with the intricate workmanship that Loki slipped the ring onto his own little finger.

As Loki took the sacks and made for the door of the smithy, Andvari shouted after him: "Go on, then, take it! Take the ring and all the gold, for it won't do you any good. I curse it all; whoever owns it will find it brings them only death!"

Turning, Loki laughed harshly and replied: "Thank you, Andvari; I will be sure to pass on your words, and the curse they contain, to those who are to receive this gold." And with that, he left Andvari's smithy and the nighted subterranean realm of the dwarfs, carrying the two bulging sacks of gold with him.

When at last Loki returned to Hreidmar's house, he found Odin and Hoenir still bound on the floor. They were very pleased to see him, although a little annoyed that he had taken so much time. Loki placed the sacks of gold in front of the other gods. "Here's the ransom for Otter . . . and" — he added in a whisper, showing the ring to Odin — "look at this. . . ."

Odin regarded its beauty and whispered back that he wanted it.

Hreidmar and his family entered the room, and seeing that the ransom had been delivered, the farmer ordered Odin and Hoenir to be released. Loki said to Hreidmar: "You will have to stuff the skin yourself." He emptied the first sack, and the farmer took the gold and stuffed the otter's skin with it, until it was bulging tightly and could contain no more. "Now we'll do the rest," Loki continued, emptying the second sack. With Odin's help, Loki piled the gold over the stuffed skin, which Hoenir held upright.

When they had finished the job, Hreidmar inspected the mound of gold. The entire skin had been covered with the exception of a single whisker, which the farmer pointed out, saying, "This, too, must be covered, otherwise I'll consider that you've broken your pledge, and your lives shall be forfeit to me."

Odin knew there and then that he would have to give up the little ring he had so prized; and so, grumbling, he took it off and placed it very carefully over the single exposed whisker, so that now the otter's skin was completely covered, with not a fragment showing.

As the three gods prepared to leave, Loki turned to Hreidmar and his family, saying, "All the gold I have given you was made by Andvari the dwarf. He wasn't too enthusiastic about my taking it from him. In fact, he placed a curse on it, which I now take pleasure in repeating to you, so that it may continue to have effect. Whoever takes possession of that gold will be destroyed by it!"

The three gods looked at each other, smiled in satisfaction, and left the farmhouse.

And what became of Hreidmar's family and their newly acquired wealth? The farmer took the gold into his possession as atonement for his son; but Fafnir and Regin desired some as atonement for their brother. Their father would hear none of this, however, and kept it all for himself; and so his sons took a dreadful course of action and killed their father. It was Regin who struck the fatal blow, and when he demanded that Fafnir divide the gold equally between them, he replied that he certainly would not give anything to the one who had killed their father, and told him to be on his way.

Fafnir took his helmet and sword and left the house. But he went up onto Gnita Heath, where he built a lair and transformed himself into a great serpent. He then lay down on the gold.

Regin became a craftsman to King Hialprek in Thiod, and became foster father to a boy named Sigurd, who was unmatched in strength and courage. Regin told Sigurd about the serpent lying on his gold, and told him to try to retrieve it from the creature. Sigurd fashioned a sword called Gram, which was so sharp it cleaved an anvil clean in two.

Sigurd and Regin went onto Gnita Heath. Sigurd dug a hole in Fafnir's path and hid there, sword in hand. When the great serpent grew thirsty and slithered down to the water to drink, passing over the hole as he did so, Sigurd thrust the sword up into his belly and killed him.

The malicious Regin then ran up to him, saying, "You have killed the serpent, but the serpent was my brother, and so now I demand atonement from you. You must take Fafnir's heart and roast it on a fire." With that, Regin himself drank some of the serpent's blood, and lay down to sleep.

Sigurd did as he was told, but when the heart was nearly cooked, he poked it with his finger to test the meat, and was scalded by the hot juice that spurted out. He put his finger to his lips, and the moment the juice entered his mouth, he found that he could understand the speech of birds. He looked up to see two tits sitting on the branch of a tree, regarding him. One of them said, "Look at Sigurd sitting there, spattered with blood. He is roasting Fafnir's heart. He would be wise to eat it himself."

The other replied, "And Regin lies there also, planning to trick poor Sigurd, who trusts him. In his anger he speaks crookedly."

Sigurd turned on Regin in rage, and killed him where he lay. He than gathered up the gold and rode away. However, in accordance with Andvari's curse, the gold did Sigurd no good, and caused him much strife and sadness.

The Gods of Light

As we have just seen, Loki was not afraid to make enemies among the other gods of the Aesir. Not least among these was Heimdall, a mysterious god about whom we know very little. He was a god of light, and may have personified both the dawn and the rainbow. In Scandinavian mythology he is depicted as being tall and very handsome, with teeth of pure gold. His function was to guard the great bridge Bifrost, which led from the world of humanity to the realm of the gods. His senses were the most subtle and finely tuned of all the gods: he could see in the dark, and his hearing was so acute that he could hear the wool growing on the backs of sheep. It was Heimdall who kept watch for the approach of the gods' enemies, and when danger approached, he would blow on his trumpet with a blasting sound that could be heard throughout the world.

Heimdall conscientiously performed his duties as guardian at the gates of Asgard, and his modesty and dependability were the causes of much hilarity for Loki, who delighted in making fun of him. Nevertheless, Heimdall could give as good as he received. When Loki stole Freyja's necklace and hid it under a reef in the western sea, it was Heimdall who went to retrieve it, transforming himself into a seal to do so. As we shall see, it also was Heimdall who ultimately killed Loki.

Balder, the son of Odin and Frigg, also was a god of light. Unmatched in beauty and wisdom, he was the favorite of the Aesir. Although he had always been happy, there came a time when Balder became deeply troubled by dreams that seemed to warn of approaching evil. When he went to the other Aesir and told them of his strange, unnamed fear, they were concerned for him. His mother asked everything on earth, living and inanimate, to swear an oath never to harm her son. Everything agreed, and from that moment on, Balder became completely invulnerable to illness and injury.

The Aesir occasionally put him to various tests by way of amusement, throwing stones at him and striking him with their weapons, none of which caused him the slightest pain or harm. All the gods were delighted at these games, with one exception: Loki. The malicious trickster hated Balder for his popularity, and resolved to find a way to harm him. Turning himself into an old woman, he visited Frigg and asked her why the gods were laughing so. She replied that

she had secured a promise from everything on earth never
to harm her son. Loki feigned surprise, and asked if she
were absolutely sure that she had overlooked nothing. Frigg
replied that there was a small plant that she had thought too
young to ask to take such a solemn oath. The plant, she said,
grew in the lands to the west of Valhalla, and was called *mis-
teltein* (mistletoe).

Loki left the goddess and went directly to the western
lands, where he gathered a branch of mistletoe. Having resumed his normal shape, he then went back to the field
where the other Aesir were continuing their game with Balder.
Only the blind god Höd was not throwing missiles. Loki
approached him and asked him why he did not join in the
game. Höd replied that it was because he could not see, and
anyway, he had no weapon.

Loki declared that this was no reason not to join in, and
handed Höd the mistletoe branch, adding that he would
guide the blind god's hand. Höd gratefully agreed, and
threw the branch at Balder. It pierced his body, and he fell to
the ground, dead. The other Aesir were stunned, and wept at
the cruel death of their beloved and beautiful friend. Then in
rage they turned to Loki, and would have fallen on him immediately had they not been standing in a part of Asgard that
had been consecrated to peace. It was the gods' own law that
no blood should be spilled here, and so instead they discussed the dreadful events among themselves.

Grief-stricken, Frigg asked if anyone would agree to descend into the kingdom of the dead to find Balder and ask
the goddess Hel to allow him to return to Asgard. Hermod,
a son of Odin, volunteered right away, and leaped on his
father's horse Sleipnir. When Hermod had departed, the
Aesir took Balder's body and placed it on a funeral pyre in his
boat. After Thor had consecrated the body with his hammer,
the boat was set on fire. They led Balder's horse into the
flames, where it was consumed along with its master.

Hermod traveled for nine days until he reached the Gjöll
River, which marked the border of the kingdom of Hel.

From the being guarding the golden bridge across the river, Hermod learned that Balder had passed this way the previous evening, escorted by five hundred warriors. Hermod continued on until he reached the gates of Hel. Pausing for only an instant, he spurred Sleipnir to jump the locked gates, and then entered the great palace of Hel, where he found Balder occupying the seat of honor.

Presenting himself to Hel, Hermod told the goddess what had happened to Balder, and begged her to allow him to leave the realm of the dead. She listened with sympathy, and told him that if everything in the world wanted Balder to return to his home in Asgard, she would indeed set him free; but should a single being fail to weep for him, she would keep him with her and never allow him to leave.

Hermod thanked the goddess of the dead and returned to Asgard to inform the other Aesir of her answer. The Aesir then sent messengers into the world to beg all the beasts and nonliving things to display their grief for Balder. This they did — men, women, animals, plants, stones, and metals. The messengers were greatly pleased with this evidently universal display of grief; but as they were returning to Asgard with the joyous news, they noticed that a single giantess was not crying, and refused to do so. Balder, she said, had never done anything for her, so now she refused to do anything for him. As far as she was concerned, she concluded, Hel was welcome to keep her prize. Crestfallen, the messengers continued on their journey home to Asgard, their good news having suddenly been transformed to bad. Of course, the giantess was actually Loki in disguise, who had thus ensured his victory over the hated Balder.

The Vanir

The Aesir had their counterparts in the Vanir, a race of peace-loving gods and goddesses who in their benevolence provided the fields and pastures with sunlight and rain. They preserved the life of the world, ensuring good harvests and all the other gifts of nature. Besides loving peace, the Vanir also were gods of commerce and navigation. According to Scandinavian mythology, they sent a goddess named Gullveig to the Aesir (the precise reason why is unknown). Gullveig was a highly skillful sorceress, and through her magical art had acquired a vast amount of gold. She made the mistake of bragging interminably to the Aesir of her enormous wealth until they grew bored, seized her, and submitted her to terrible tortures. First they pierced her body with spears and then threw her onto the fire in the middle of Odin's hall. Her body was completely destroyed in the flames; but to the Aesir's surprise, she stepped out of the fire, rejuvenated. They tried to burn her again and again, but each time she proved herself capable of stepping from the flames unharmed.

When the Vanir heard what had happened, they were outraged, and demanded that the Aesir make amends immediately, either by paying them huge reparations, or recognizing the Vanir as possessing equal stature to the Aesir. The warlike Aesir decided that the most satisfactory way of settling the matter would be to fight.

There followed a long and violent war between the two races of gods, and although the Vanir were kind and benevolent, they acquitted themselves extremely well, winning many engagements against their battle-loving opponents. Eventually the equally matched sides came to an understanding, with the Aesir agreeing to treat the Vanir as equals. To cement the agreement, each side turned over a number of hostages to the other: the Aesir sent Hoenir and Mimir; and the Vanir sent Njörd and his son Frey.

The giant Thiazi, who had been burned to death as an eagle following his failed attempt to imprison the goddess Idun, had a daughter named Skadi, who vowed to take her revenge on the Aesir. However, when she tried to attack them, they told her that they did not want to fight against a woman, and instead offered her the choice of a member of

the Aesir to take as a husband. The gods hid themselves behind a curtain that left only their feet visible. Skadi was desperate to obtain Balder, so she studied the Aesir's feet intently,
trying to remember by their shape which feet belonged to
each god. Finally, however, she made the wrong choice: the
curtain was drawn aside to reveal not Balder, but Njörd.

Skadi did not renege on the agreement; she married
Njörd, but told him that she wanted to live in the mountainous realm of her ancestors. Although he agreed to go with
her, after a few days Njörd confessed that the howling of the
wolves annoyed him, and that he preferred the sweet singing
of the swans in his own lands. Skadi replied that she felt the
same way about the sharp cries of the seabirds, so they
agreed that it would be better to live apart.

The couple had a son, Frey, who possessed many magical
objects, including a horse that could cover any terrain at
lightning speed; a sword that guided itself to its target; and a
golden boar (forged by the dwarfs Brökk and Sindri) that
could draw his chariot faster than any horse. In addition, he
possessed the boat *Skidbladnir,* which would take its crew to
any destination as soon as they raised its sails. When in use,
Skidbladnir could accommodate all the Aesir, and yet it also
could be folded up and carried in Frey's pocket.

Frey fell helplessly in love with a giantess named Gerda,
who was daughter of Gymir. Unable to think of a way to win
her, Frey grew deeply unhappy, and his concerned parents
asked their faithful friend and servant Skirnir to find out
what troubled their son so. Skirnir readily agreed, and when
Frey told him of his desperate love for Gerda, Skirnir offered
to go to her himself and ask for her hand on Frey's behalf. To
aid him in his mission, Skirnir asked to borrow Frey's self-
guiding sword and his wondrous horse.

Skirnir departed that night, and headed for the realm of
the giants. As he approached Gymir's palace, he saw that it
was guarded by vicious dogs and was surrounded by a protective shield of fire. Skirnir was undaunted, for the horse
was impervious to fire. He vaulted the flames and rode straight

through the wall of the palace. Attracted by the sudden commotion, Gerda appeared, and Skirnir delivered the message from Frey, along with eleven golden apples and the ring Draupnir.

Skirnir had his work cut out, for Gerda was singularly unimpressed with the secondhand declaration of love. Skirnir unsheathed the self-guiding sword and brandished it threateningly, but Gerda remained unmoved. Somewhat at a loss in the face of this intransigence, Skirnir put the sword away and tried a different, though still threatening, strategy. He told her he had found a magic wand in the forest, and added that unless she went with him, he would carve runes on it that would transport her to the far side of the world, where she would live alone, far from men.

This had the desired effect: Gerda was now very frightened, and offered Skirnir a cup of mead as a token of her acceptance of Frey. Impatiently the messenger refused the cup, demanding that she accompany him immediately. She refused, but promised to meet Frey in nine days' time in a certain sacred grove.

Unfortunately, we do not know how this love story ended, for the poems in which it was undoubtedly completed have not survived. It is likely that Frey did win Gerda's heart, but only after some physical trial involving combat with the giants. Whatever feat he was required to perform, it seems that Frey lost his sword, for in the great war between the gods and the giants that heralded the end of the world, Frey fought without his magical weapon and consequently fell in battle.

Minor Gods and Goddesses

The Aesir were not the only gods to appear in the Scandinavian legends. There was a whole host of minor deities who contributed to the creation of the world and who accompanied the Aesir on their numerous adventures. One of these minor gods was Hoenir, whom we have already met. Brave and handsome but not particularly intelligent, Hoenir was credited with breathing souls into the bodies of the first humans. The following tale illustrates the role played by Hoenir in the exploits of more famous gods such as Odin and Loki.

A giant forced a peasant to play a game of checkers with him. The loser would forfeit his life. When the peasant won, the giant immediately suggested a bargain: if the peasant allowed him to live, the giant would build him a magnificent house and fill it with all manner of goods and provisions. The peasant agreed, and by the following day the giant had built a truly palatial residence, into which the peasant and his family happily moved.

However, the giant was not finished with the peasant, and persuaded him to play another game of checkers. This time, should the peasant lose, he would have to give his son to the giant, unless he found a way of concealing the boy. The peasant lost, and was faced with the awful problem of successfully hiding his son from the giant's gaze. In desperation, he turned to Odin, who caused a field of barley to instantly appear. He then transformed the boy into a grain of barley and placed him within one of the ears.

The giant arrived, and cut down the entire field of barley, striking each ear with his sword to find the boy. When the grain he was looking for slipped from the giant's hand, Odin quickly took it away and returned it to the peasant and his wife. Regretfully, he informed them that this was all he would be able to do for them.

Grateful but still in abject fear for his son's safety, the peasant went to Hoenir for help. The god took the boy to the seashore, where he found two swans. Hoenir then transformed him into a feather, which he placed on the head of one of the great white birds. But without warning the giant appeared, grabbed the bird, and wrung its neck. As with the grain of barley, the feather he was looking for slipped from his grasp and floated away. Hoenir restored the boy to his human form and returned him to his parents, regretfully stating that, like Odin, he could offer no more help.

Finally the peasant turned to Loki, and the wily god hatched a scheme to rid the peasant and his family of the troublesome giant once and for all. He transformed the boy into one of the eggs in a turbot's roe. When the giant appeared and caught the fish, he examined the roe, but once again the egg he was seeking slipped through his fingers. The boy resumed his human form and ran as fast as he could across the beach. Infuriated, the giant cast the turbot aside and ran blindly after him, stumbling into the trap Loki had prepared for him. The giant died, and the boy was finally free to return to his family.

The Scandinavians occasionally modified their mythology, as with another minor god, Bragi, who, as we have seen, incurred Loki's wrath at Aegir's banquet. The poet Bragi Boddason lived in the ninth century, and was greatly admired for his invention of a certain type of poetic form. Historians believe that, following his death, Bragi Boddason was deified and joined the Aesir in Asgard, where he married the goddess Idun. He was assigned the duty of welcoming dead warriors to Valhalla, and of entertaining them in the evenings with stories of the adventures of the gods.

Vidar and Vali are two of the most obscure of the other gods. Vidar was Odin's son, and since he spoke very little, was regarded as being perhaps a little stupid. Nevertheless, he was a formidable warrior, and his bravery was immortalized in his slaying of the wolf Fenrir. Vidar also survived the bloody war between the gods and the giants, and witnessed the transition from the Old World to the New. Vali also was Odin's son, and was only one day old when he swore to make Höd pay for the death of Balder. (This seems a little unfair since, as we have seen, Höd was really a victim of Loki's wickedness.)

The god Ull (Magnificent) was Thor's stepson. Ull was a supremely skilled huntsman, and was so noble that the Aesir chose him to replace Odin for a while as leader of the gods. Odin had been accused of using underhanded methods to seduce a maiden, and had been banished by the others. Odin stayed away for ten years, but then returned and reclaimed his leadership by driving Ull away. Ull then left the Aesir and went to live in Sweden, where he gained a reputation as a powerful magician. It was said that he owned a bone on which he had carved runes of such power that they enabled him to use the bone as a ship to cross the seas.

Although living somewhat in the background of Scandinavian legend, the goddesses were nevertheless both numerous and important. Frigg was Odin's wife, and she accompanied him on a number of his adventures. She was his equal in wisdom, and there were times when they disagreed quite vehemently with each other, especially with regard to which warriors should fall in battle and which should be allowed to survive. There also were many occasions when she was unfaithful to Odin (and he to her, of course), whether through self-interest or mere lust, and she was believed to have consorted with many other gods.

The goddess Freyja belonged to the race known as the Vanir, the great rivals of the Aesir. Although she usually is distinguished from Frigg in the literature of ancient Scandinavia, some legends identify them with each other, describing Freyja also as the wife of Odin. Freyja lived in the sky in a marvelous palace called Folkvang, where she welcomed dead heroes. She was the commander of the Valkyries, and was entitled to claim half of those who fell in battle.

Not far from Freyja's palace lived four dwarfs who were much renowned for their skill in metalworking. Freyja loved jewelery, and one day when she was visiting the dwarfs in the grotto they used as their workshop, she noticed an incredibly beautiful golden necklace to which they were about to put the finishing touches. Freyja decided that she had to have the necklace, and offered to pay the dwarfs in gold and silver. They laughed at this offer, and replied that she could have the necklace only if she agreed to spend a night with each of them. Freyja regarded the ugly, misshapen dwarfs with the greatest distaste. She certainly had no desire to sleep with one of them, let alone all. However, she had even less desire to leave without the beautiful necklace, and so, reluctantly, she agreed and, having paid the unpleasant price, took the necklace back to her palace.

Loki witnessed the transaction and, ever on the lookout for new mischief to cause, went straight to Odin and told him what Freyja had done. The leader of the gods was outraged, and told Loki to steal the necklace. The trickster god immediately went to Freyja's bedchamber, but found the door locked. Transforming himself into a fly, he buzzed around looking for a way to enter, and eventually discovered a tiny hole in the roof through which he could squeeze.

Freyja was asleep, but was lying in such a way that Loki could not reach the clasp of the necklace, so he changed into a flea and bit the goddess on the cheek. Disturbed but not awoken, Freyja turned over, revealing the clasp. Loki then resumed his normal form, carefully unclasped the necklace, and stole silently from the chamber.

When Freyja awoke and discovered the theft, she was furious. Guessing right away who was responsible, she went to Odin and demanded that he return the necklace. There followed a heated argument in which Odin made clear his displeasure at the manner in which Freyja had obtained the trinket. Eventually he consented to return it, but only on certain conditions. Freyja, he said, would have to provoke a war between two human kings, each of whom commanded twenty lesser kings. During each night of the war, she would have to restore to life those who had fallen in battle, so that the war would continue the following day with all fighters returned to their former condition. Freyja would not receive her necklace until a Christian warrior arrived to defeat all the pagans. (Historians believe that this element in the story was the result of the later influence of Christianity on the Norse poets.) Eventually a Christian did arrive to defeat the pagan warriors, and Odin returned his wife's ill-gotten necklace to her.

As we have seen, Freyja is sometimes identified with the goddess Frigg; Freyja also is identified with a fertility goddess named Gefjon (Giver). Gefjon was worshiped on an island called Sjælland, and there is a particularly charming legend that explains the origin of the cult devoted to her. An ancient king named Gylfi was delighted by the magical arts of a mysterious, wandering woman. As a reward, Gylfi offered to give her as much land as she could mark out in a day and a night with a plow drawn by four bullocks. What Gylfi did not know was that the woman was actually the goddess Gefjon, who had been taught the magical arts by the Vanir. She had four sons, whose father was a giant, and whom she transformed into bullocks to draw her plow. So powerful were these "bullocks" that the plow they drew tore away the very crust of the earth and dragged it into the sea, where it became the island of Sjælland. The vast hollow in the land left behind gradually filled with water and became a lake, known today in Sweden as Lake Mälar.

We have already met the goddess Hel, and although there are few legends concerning her, she remains a fascinating deity, not least because her attributes were influenced by Christian ideas following the conversion of the Norse lands. She was believed to be the daughter of Loki, whom the later legends identified with Lucifer. Hel spent her childhood in the realm of the giants, in the company of the wolf Fenrir and the world serpent of Midgard. She had many other terrifying monsters for her companions, including Nidhögg, who gnawed incessantly at the roots of the world tree Yggdrasil. Notwithstanding these fearsome companions, Hel herself was not considered an irredeemably evil deity. Her appearance, however, was strange to the point of frightfulness: her face was half human, half totally featureless. She dwelled in a vast palace in the shadowy realm of Niflheim, where she received all those — humans or gods — who descended to her domain. Hel's palace was not a place of punishment, like the Christian hell; in fact, it was very similar to Valhalla, with fallen warriors being honored with great feasts. She is perhaps the most mysterious of the Norse deities, dwelling apart from the other gods, a queen of eternal shadows.

Other Supernatural Beings

In common with many other ancient cultures, the Vikings held the spirits of the dead in reverence and more than a little fear. They believed that spirits were very powerful, and could use magical powers for good or ill. When a person died, his or her soul frequently remained close to its place of burial, and for this reason people often were buried close to the family home, so their souls might give protection to the surviving relatives.

Interestingly, the Germanic peoples believed that the soul could occasionally leave the body of a healthy person and act independently for short periods, an ancient precursor of the "out-of-body experiences" with which most people are familiar today. The Scandinavians called this entity the *fylgja* (plural, *fylgjur*), which is roughly translated as "the follower" or "the second." Although the *fylgja* could leave the physical body, it nevertheless felt any injury that befell the body; and when the body died, so did the *fylgja*.

Once outside the body, the *fylgja* could assume other forms, and this led to the belief that certain people could transform themselves into animals. The werewolf legend has its origin here, although it was conceded that werewolves were themselves occasionally victims, the unwanted ability resulting from the sorcery of one's enemy.

Such sorcery is described in the story of Sigmund and Sinfjöth, who came upon a cabin in a forest. Inside were two men, fast asleep. Two wolf skins hung on a wall. The men were the victims of a sorcerer who had turned them into wolves. Their only respite from the curse was the ability to leave the wolf skins every ten days and return to human form for a single day. Sigmund and Sinfjöth took the skins and placed them on their own backs; but to their horror they found that they could not take them off again. They had been transformed into ravenous wolves. The curse had been transferred to them; it was now they who were compelled to take the forms of wolves for periods of ten days, with only one day in between spent as humans. They were smarter than the previous victims, however, for at the end of the first ten days, they took off the wolf skins and burned them, thus breaking the curse.

Belief in the *fylgjur* gradually developed until they came to be seen as entirely independent entities, which took the form of armed women. With the conversion to Christianity, they were transformed from protective spirits to evil demons. The story of the Icelander Thidrandi illustrates this transition. Thidrandi heard a knock on his door one night. Assuming that someone was about to attack his home, he grabbed his sword, threw open his door, and strode out into the darkness. He was confronted with the sight of nine strange women dressed in black, riding toward him from the north, with swords drawn. Turning around, he saw nine more women approaching from the south; but these were dressed in white and were riding white horses. Suddenly terrified, Thidrandi turned and made for his house. But he was too late: the women in black descended on him, striking fatal blows with their swords.

Thidrandi was discovered the following morning, lying by his door and on the very edge of death. With his final breath he managed to tell his fellows what had happened. According to the interpretation of these strange events, the black *fylgjur* were spirits who had retained their paganism, while the white had converted to Christianity. The black spirits had agreed to accept Christianity, but only on the condition that they were granted a last sacrifice — the unfortunate Thidrandi.

Some spirits could alter the destiny of humans. In Scandinavia they were called the Norns, and were seen as wise women who spin the destinies of humans from the threads they hold in their hands. Such was their power that the Norns sat in judgment on both men and gods, deciding on the destinies they would be forced to follow.

Urd was the first and wisest of the Norns; the name was derived from the Old Norse *urdr,* meaning "fate." Soon she was joined by several sisters, some of whom did their best to increase human happiness, while others were malignant, and went out of their way to cause misfortune and vexation. The Norns later gave rise to the legends of the fairies who would appear at the cradle of a newborn child, and either offer it gifts or pronounce curses that would blight the rest of its life.

An example of this is the Scandinavian legend of the hero Nornagest, at whose cradle three prophetesses appeared. As two candles burned serenely nearby, the first two women looked benevolently down on the child and announced that they had bestowed virtues on him that would ensure happiness for his whole life. But in their desire to see the baby, the people crowded around the cradle and jostled the third prophetess to the floor. Enraged at this maltreatment, the woman rose to her feet and announced that she would punish the child for the bad manners of the others. She cried that at the moment the candle nearest to him ran out, so, too, would his life be extinguished. The oldest of the three women instantly seized the candle, snuffed out its flame, and told the child's mother not to light it again until her son's final day. The child was named Nornagest, "the guest, protected by the Norns."

Those familiar with J. R. R. Tolkien's wonderful adventure novel *The Lord of the Rings* will know of the many exploits of elves and dwarfs (and other races besides). Tolkien was greatly inspired by the myths and legends of the northern lands, and elves and dwarfs figure prominently throughout. Although the modern image of the elf is of a graceful, slender, and very beautiful being with long hair, pointed ears, and a staggering proficiency with a bow and arrow, the original definition of the word included all the spirits and demons inhabiting the world of nature. They were highly ambivalent beings, who could be either helpful and kind, or evil and vindictive. We owe our present beliefs about elves to the English poets of the Middle Ages, who invariably described them as beautiful and benevolent.

The society of elves was organized along lines similar to those of humans, with kings, queens, and subjects. One of their greatest loves was dancing, and they would think nothing of dancing all night long, only ceasing at daybreak, for they disliked sunlight. It was considered extremely inadvisable to watch them dancing in their forest clearings, and any traveler who chanced upon them would only have to glance at the exquisite faces of the female elves to be helplessly enchanted. Should the elves manage to persuade the traveler to join in their dance, he would be lost forever to his own world and would never be seen by humans again.

Dwarfs were related to elves, but were very different in appearance, being small, stocky, with large heads and long, thick beards. Like the elves, they possessed superhuman intelligence, and had the gift of foresight. They preferred to live in the secret places of the world, especially in underground caverns. There are many tales told of miners encountering dwarfs in the deep galleries below mountains, the dwarfs themselves engaged in mining activities. Indeed, mining was one of their greatest skills, and they knew where the most precious and useful metals could be found far underground. Thus, far from being afraid of them, human miners often hoped they would run into a group of dwarfs, for to do so meant that rich veins were near at hand.

The giants with whom the Viking gods so often did battle were very similar to the dwarfs and elves in terms of their personalities and exploits. The main difference, of course, was their size. Like their small cousins, giants could be either friendly or hostile, but their immense power invariably inspired fear and respect.

According to Scandinavian legend, the giants were the

very first creatures to appear on the earth. They were older even than the gods. The giants carried with them much of the brutality of the world that had newly emerged from the primeval abyss, and their attributes were closely identified with those of untamed nature. They were seen in storm clouds, and the thunder was said to carry their mighty voices.

Nor were the giants afraid of the gods; in fact, the giants delighted in provoking and fighting with them. On one occasion, a giant named Geirröd invited Thor to his castle, and there challenged him to a duel in which the loser would be bound to the will of the victor. With a pair of enormous tongs, Geirröd withdrew a lump of red-hot iron from his fire, and told his guest that they would take turns throwing it at each other. When Thor agreed, the giant hurled the molten iron at him. He caught it with ease in his iron gloves, much to the surprise of Geirröd, who had expected Thor to be killed instantly. The giant now thought better of his idea, and ran to hide behind one of his castle's titanic iron pillars. But he could not hope to defeat the thunder god. With all his might, Thor hurled the lump of iron, which smashed through the pillar, the giant, and the wall of the castle before coming to rest on the ground outside.

There were giants in the sea as well as on the land. One of the most important sea giants in Scandinavian mythology was Aegir, who was a friend to the gods, and often invited them to the great feasts he held in his undersea palace. Aegir had a wife, Ran (Ravisher), who owned a magical net with which she would attempt to snare any man who set out on the seas. It was Ran who made the waters rough and treacherous, and so great and fearsome was her power that in the minds of the Vikings she grew in importance, becoming more a goddess than a giantess. Those who died at sea had little to fear from her, however, for she welcomed the drowned in her palace and presented them with enormous feasts of fish.

The belief in these supernatural beings did not die out with the conversion to Christianity. In fact, the two traditions were occasionally amalgamated, as with the story of how the Christian converter Olaf Tryggvason forced a giant to build him a church. This story is typical of a certain kind of legend in which the Christian tricks the supernatural being (in other words, the devil) into constructing a building on the promise that the entity will be rewarded with a human sacrifice. Once the building is completed, the Christian finds a way to outwit the demon, who then withdraws in anger and frustration.

Perhaps the strangest legends are those in which the demons themselves desire conversion to Christianity. In one of these tales, two children were playing beside a river close to their father's house. Suddenly a water spirit emerged from the river and began to play a beautiful tune on his harp. The children were unimpressed, and informed the spirit that even a talent such as his would not bring him salvation. At this, the spirit wept, threw away his harp, and sank once again into the river.

The children returned to the house and told their father what had happened. Even though he was a pastor, their father was very angry with them for having caused a friendly spirit such sadness, and told them to go back to the river and assure the water spirit that he would indeed be accepted into the kingdom of heaven. When they returned to the river, the children found the water spirit sitting on the waves, still weeping. They called out to him, reassuring him and telling him that Jesus came to earth for him as well. On hearing their words, the spirit dried his tears, took up his harp again, and resumed playing his beautiful music.

This is a rather charming example of how the Vikings saw different spiritual beliefs as complementary rather than as mutually exclusive. When they settled in Britain and Ireland in the ninth century, they saw nothing wrong with adopting the religion of those lands while retaining belief in their own gods and goddesses. For this reason it took hundreds of years for the Scandinavians to leave their paganism behind, although the stories retain their power to fascinate even today.

The Doom of the Gods

The Vikings did not believe that either the world or the gods would last forever. They had to be constantly on their guard against the many other supernatural beings who struggled to usurp their power. Not for nothing did Heimdall stand guard on Bifrost, the bridge that gave access to Asgard. The final battle that saw the defeat and destruction of the Aesir is recounted in the Völuspa, and is known as Ragnarök, from *ragna rök,* "the doom of the gods." However, the battle is, of course, also known as the Götterdämmerung, "the twilight of the gods." This came about as a result of twelfth-century Norse writers who altered the original expression to *ragna rökkr,* meaning "shadows" or "twilight."

The Aesir began their lives in peace and prosperity, building their gigantic palaces, spending their days playing checkers and enjoying their beautiful possessions. This age of peace might have lasted forever had not the Aesir succumbed to their passions. As we have seen, the first celestial war began after they tortured Gullveig, the emissary from the Vanir, to stifle her relentless bragging about her treasure.

One of their greatest mistakes was to break their word to the giant they employed to rebuild their dwellings. As payment, they had promised him the goddess Freyja; but when the giant had completed his colossal labors, the Aesir instructed Loki to perform a deceit that robbed the giant of his prize. This had a far-reaching effect, for from that moment on, all the treaties and agreements made all over the world began to lose their force and validity. This was the beginning of a fall from innocence that afflicted all the gods, giants, and humans, who descended into a dreadful morass of hatred and violence. As warfare raged across the face of the world, Odin listened to the Aesir recount the strange and terrifying dreams from which they had begun to suffer, and understood that a titanic battle was inexorably approaching. Other shadows were gathering in the East, where an ancient giantess gave birth to a brood of wolves whose father was Fenrir. One of these wolves chased the sun, growing in strength with each passing season until finally he caught it and extinguished its rays. For many years the world suffered in the grip of a terrible winter. Wars continued to scar the landscape as human beings became as animals, falling on each other like wolves and reveling in blood and pain. And all the while, the world moved toward the primeval abyss of nonexistence from which it had emerged.

While humans slaughtered each other, the warrior Eggther, watchman of the giants, stood guard at the edge of his kingdom, silently regarding the violence as it spread like a disease through the lands of men and gods. At the border of the underworld the demon dog Garm howled madly, calling to battle all those spirits of the dead who were under his command. In the realm of the fire giants, the warrior lord Surt raised his sword of fire and prepared to enter the fray.

Meanwhile, Loki, who had turned on his fellows and was now fighting the Aesir on the side of their enemies, stole Heimdall's sword, leaving the watchman of the Aesir defenseless. As the giants began to march on Asgard, Heimdall blew his great horn, the baleful sound alerting the other gods to the approaching peril. The wolf Fenrir, whom the Aesir had successfully bound with their magical chain, broke free and escaped. As the chain broke, the whole earth trembled and the mountains shook. Even Yggdrasil, the great ash tree that was the axis of the universe, trembled, from its roots to the tips of its branches. The mountains also shook and shuddered, so that the entrances to the homes of the dwarfs disappeared, causing panic and consternation among their ranks.

The giant Hrym arrived from the West to do battle, on a ship manned by a crew of ghosts, carried forward on great waves caused by the world serpent of Midgard. From the North came another ship, carrying the denizens of the underworld and commanded by Loki. Fenrir stood at his side, with flames leaping from his nostrils and blood dripping from his jaws. When he opened his mouth, his gaping jaws reached from the earth to the heavens.

An army of fire giants came from the South, led by Surt, whose great sword disgorged forks of lightning that fell on the earth, igniting everything they touched. At his approach, men fell dead in an instant, and the ground on which they had stood split open, revealing roiling flames beneath. With ease they took the bridge connecting the earth with Asgard, and as they passed, the bridge caught fire and collapsed.

The field of battle was called Vigrid, which extended for millions of square miles before the hall of Valhalla. From the great Hall of the Slain the Aesir charged forth, led by Odin, who wore a great golden helmet surmounted by eagles' wings and who carried the self-guiding spear Gungnir. Above him flew the Valkyries on their celestial steeds. In spite of his strength and bravery, it was Odin who perished first. He had spotted Fenrir among the ranks of the enemy, and had flown at him with his sword whipping through the air in deadly arcs. But the wolf opened his vast jaws and swallowed the Allfather in a single titanic gulp.

On seeing his father's death, Odin's son Vidar immediately took his vengeance on Fenrir. Striding up to the gigantic wolf, Vidar placed one foot on his lower jaw, fixing it to the ground, while with his right hand he raised the upper jaw to the sky. Vidar's shoes were made from indestructible leather, and so they were impervious to the wolf's razor-sharp fangs. With Fenrir now helpless before him, Vidar took his sword and plunged it down the wolf's throat, piercing his heart and killing him.

The thunder god Thor spied an old adversary among the enemy: the world serpent of Midgard, which he had once tried to kill, but had been frustrated by the cowardice of the giant Hymir. Now the serpent had left behind a sea poisoned by the torrents of putrid venom it had spat in its rage and hatred. It crawled across the land toward the gods, spitting more venom, which turned the air poisonous. Thor would not be denied satisfaction a second time, and advanced toward his foe. With a single swing of his mighty hammer, Thor crushed the serpent's skull; but as the dying beast fell away from him, Thor felt his strength leaving him. He had breathed in too much of the poison; he tried to stagger away, but instead fell to the ground, dead.

Other scores were settled on that dreadful day. Loki fell on his old enemy Heimdall and killed him, but lost his own life in doing so. Frey met Surt, chief of the fire giants, in battle but was forced to fight without his magical sword, which he had lost during his successful attempt to win the hand of the giantess Gerda. Now Surt carried the sword, and with it he killed the valiant Frey.

As the great battle drew toward its climax, only one of the Aesir was left alive. Tyr strode across the battlefield, hoping to find and take revenge on Fenrir, who had once bitten off his right hand. He was too late, of course, for Fenrir already lay dead. However, another adversary soon presented itself to Tyr: the demon dog Garm, howling madly. Tyr threw himself on the infernal beast and with his left hand plunged his sword into its heart. But the creature mauled the god so frightfully that he, too, died.

With all the gods now dead, including Thor, the protector of humanity, their enemies descended on the earth and drove humanity from it. The destruction of the universe had begun; as the earth buckled and split open, the stars themselves were decoupled from the sky and drifted off into the primeval void from which all had issued at the beginning of time. The fire giant Surt set the wounded earth ablaze; the flames spread, and soon the entire universe was an immense furnace. All life was extinguished, and both the earth and the sky were reduced to blasted wastelands split by cracks and fissures. The seas boiled and foamed, their waves crashing insanely on each other, until the earth and the domain of the gods became completely submerged.

But then, slowly, from the wreckage of the universe a new world began to emerge. The waves eventually subsided, and mountains rose from the watery depths. Bright rivers cascaded from the mountainsides, above which eagles hovered, ready to swoop down on the fish that swam through them. The fields became green again, and corn sprouted plentifully, even though no one had survived to sow any seeds. And high in the sky, a new sun, offspring of the old that had been devoured, shone in serene glory.

The old gods were dead; but in their place arose a new generation of gods, who had existed previously but had never become involved with the violent hatreds and intrigues that had afflicted the old ones. The beautiful and beloved Balder was resurrected, and occupied the great hall that had once belonged to Odin. Two of Odin's sons, Vidar and Vali, and two of his nephews, Vili and Ve, now took up residence in the sky. Hoenir also survived, and now devoted himself to studying the runes on magic wands, which revealed to him the course of future events. The new pantheon of gods was completed by Thor's sons Magni and Modi.

Presently the race of humans also reappeared on the earth. Although vast numbers had perished, some had sought refuge within the wood of Yggdrasil, which the flames of Ragnarök had been unable to harm. In this way the world was repopulated.

3

Society and Culture

At home a man should be cheerful and merry with his guest,
he should be shrewd about himself,
with a good memory and eloquent, if he wants to be very
* wise,*
often should he speak of good things;
a nincompoop that man is called, who can't say much for
* himself,*
that is the hallmark of a fool.
                                          — *Sayings of the High One*

The People and Their Settlements

The popular notion of the Vikings as savage and bloodthirsty conquerors, pillagers, and pirates is far from complete. While it is certainly true that the sight of their longships brought terror to the hearts of the people of England, Ireland, France, and elsewhere, there was much more to Viking life and culture than the slash of the battle-ax. In this chapter we will concentrate on the everyday life of the Vikings — the way they lived, dressed, traded, hunted, and fished, their homes, family life, and the way they entertained themselves. We will see that there really was a gentler side to Scandinavian society, which tempered the often violent desire to expand into new lands.

Scandinavia is a very beautiful part of the world, yet it can be a terribly unforgiving environment. To live off the land in these spectacular northern realms required a special blend of toughness, resilience, and also the willingness and ability to cooperate and look out for one's fellows. In Norway and Sweden the winter ice lasts for months, holding the land in a grip of cold iron. The Vikings built their villages in the places where Nature offered the most protection from the snow, ice, and biting winds of winter. The coastal fjords offered the best shelter and the most secure harbors, particularly along the western coast of Norway, where the warmer waters of the Gulf Stream prevent the encroachment of ice during the long winter months.

Viking families were close-knit: parents, grandparents, and children lived in the same home. The typical Viking house had one main room, at the center of which stood the fireplace. There was a hole in the roof directly above, through which the smoke could escape. Other rooms, such as kitchens and weaving rooms, were added to the main structure. The family was of paramount importance, and this is reflected in the Viking laws regarding the inheritance of property. Land and property were kept within the kin.

In the settled parts of Scandinavia, farming activity was given over mainly to animal husbandry. The Vikings raised various animals, including cattle, goats, pigs, and sheep. In the more southerly regions, where the land was more conducive to raising crops, they grew barley, peas, beans, rye, oats, and cabbages. North of Denmark and southern Sweden, the land was harder to farm; nevertheless, there were vast stocks of fish and wild animals, and these formed an important part of the Viking economy, together with valuable goods from the Arctic, such as fur and pelts.

In Denmark, the southernmost country in Scandinavia, people tended to live in small villages. Archaeological evidence suggests that these villages were not permanent settlements: they were abandoned every century or so in favor of new sites. Permanent settlements did not appear until after the Viking Age had ended. Norway was altogether a tougher place to live, with far less fertile land than in Denmark, so people in Norway tended to live a comparatively isolated existence in small farmsteads that clung precariously to the unforgiving land. In Sweden, to the east, settlement was likewise confined to small farms scattered here and there in the few small tracts of cultivable land — for instance, in the regions of Västergötland and Uppland. Throughout the Viking Age the population of Scandinavia steadily increased, and this contributed in no small part to the development of villages as people constantly sought new land to farm on, laying claim to suitable areas among the established settlements.

The typical Viking Age farm consisted of a main building, or longhouse, in which the people lived with their animals. This was surrounded by a number of other buildings with various functions, such as workshops or storehouses. Some smaller buildings were half buried, their floors sunk into the ground. The function of these is uncertain, but they probably were used to store perishable items that needed to be kept cool.

The type of construction the Vikings used for their buildings depended on where they lived, and the resources available in their immediate environment. In forested areas, such as in Norway and Sweden, they took advantage of the plentiful timber, and built their houses with stout wooden walls and floors. The roofs were composites of waterproof birch bark and turf for insulation. Farther to the south there were far fewer trees from which to build dwellings, so timber was used only as a framework; the walls were constructed of clay-plastered wattle, and the roofs were thatched. The Vikings who settled Iceland, which was treeless, had no option but to build their dwellings from turf and stone.

There were numerous villages in Jutland, the best known of which is Vorbasse, which is the most extensively excavated farming village. The history of the many stages of this little settlement dates all the way back to 100 B.C. Between A.D. 700 and 1000 the village contained six farms of roughly equal size, each of which had about twenty cows. The farmers also grew grain, and it is likely that they managed to produce a surplus, which they could trade for various items they needed but did not have the resources to produce for themselves. These might have included timber for building, whetstones, and good pottery. The farms themselves were all of a similar layout: the plots were large and roughly square in shape, with a wide gateway leading to the public thoroughfare. The main building stood more or less in the center of the plot, with smaller buildings standing close to the inside of the fence surrounding the farm. Most of the farms had wells, and one had a smithy, at the edge of the settlement to minimize the risk of fire.

Rules of Conduct

Viking society was bound by a code of morality and personal conduct, and the most precious thing a man could possess was his good name, his honor. Loyalty was of extreme importance, to one's family, and also to one's *félag*, or fellowship, be it in business, trade, or warfare. Personal honor was strongly associated with qualities one might not at first think of in the stereotypical Viking barbarian. Physical courage and skill in battle were, of course, of great importance, but so were magnanimity and generosity, eloquence and self-control. Following the conversion to Christianity, it also was thought worthy to undertake construction projects for the benefit of society, such as church-building.

The rules of Viking conduct are preserved in a poem called "Hávamál" (The Words of the High One), one of the thirty-nine poems in the *Edda*, compiled in Iceland in the thirteenth century. "Hávamál" is a collection of maxims offering down-to-earth advice on how to live one's life and deal honorably with one's fellows. Although they are more than a thousand years old, many of these maxims contain good advice for the present:

Look carefully around doorways before you walk in; you never know when an enemy might be there.

There is no better load a man can carry than much common sense; no worse a load than too much drink.

Never part with your weapons when out in the fields; you never know when you will need your spear.

Be a friend to your friend, match gift with gift; meet smiles with smiles, and lies with dissimulation.

No need to give too much to a man, a little can buy much thanks; with half a loaf and a tilted jug I often won me a friend.

Confide in one, never in two; confide in three, and the whole world knows.

Praise no day until evening, no wife until buried, no sword until tested, no maid until bedded, no ice until crossed, no ale until drunk.

The halt can ride, the handless can herd, the deaf can fight with spirit; a blind man is better than a corpse on a pyre — a corpse is no good to anyone.

Wealth dies, kinsmen die, a man himself must likewise die; but word fame never dies for him who achieves it well.

The tactful guest will leave early and not linger long; he starts to stink who outstays his welcome.

It is best for a man to be fairly wise, not overly cunning and clever; no man can know his future, so let him sleep peacefully.

Not all sick men are utterly wretched; some are blessed with sons, some with friends, some with riches, some with worthy works.

Women and Children

Women played an important part in Viking society, not least because it was their responsibility to run the home while their husbands were on military expeditions or trading voyages. In

Viking Age Scandinavia, men and women had separate and very clearly defined roles: the men tended the land, hunted, fished, traded, and launched attacks on other lands; the women spun wool, baked bread, churned butter, ground grain, made clothes, and looked after the children. There is plenty of evidence that women's efforts were appreciated, as can be seen from the obituaries given by their husbands. In Västmanland, Sweden, a woman named Odindisa was missed greatly by her husband, who had it written: "There will not come to Hassmyra a better mistress who holds sway over the farm." The objects found in Viking graves reflect this division in society. In the graves of men are found weapons, hunting dogs, tools, and other objects befitting their role; in those of women are found domestic items such as lapdogs, jewelry, and needles and other weaving equipment. Women's graves were as impressive as those of men; in *The Vikings* Else Roesdahl notes that the woman's grave at Oseberg, southern Norway, is "the most magnificently furnished of all Viking Age graves."

Viking marriages usually were arranged between the suitor and the woman's father, although the woman herself usually was consulted and her wishes taken into account. Marriage was considered an alliance between equals, with the bride bringing a dowry, and the husband paying her a "bride-price," both of which she retained after the marriage. There also was a marriage contract that stipulated how the couple's property should be divided in the event of divorce, which women had the right to instigate. While they had no influence on public life, women exercised great authority within the home, and their views were sought when decisions needed to be made regarding the family.

Viking women took the honor of the family as seriously as the men, and did not hesitate to encourage taking revenge for any injury or transgression. Adultery received very harsh punishment for men as well as women: adulterers were executed, while adulteresses were sold as slaves.

Although Viking women did not fight alongside their men-folk, some warriors in the armies fighting in western Europe in the late ninth century did take their wives and children with them. They would doubtless have performed useful roles as cooks and nurses for the wounded.

Women played an even more important role in the Viking settlements of Iceland and Greenland, and enjoyed a higher status than at home in Scandinavia. In Vinland, also, they contributed greatly to the attempt to settle the new land, and their participation is recorded in the sagas commemorating that period of high adventure and hardship.

The position of women in Viking society is further illustrated by the fact that royal descent on the mother's side allowed a legitimate claim to the throne. Else Roesdahl writes in *The Vikings:*

> Svein Estridsson (1047–74), for example, fought for the Danish crown on the basis of his legal right, derived from his mother Estrid, who was the daughter of Svein Fork-Beard and sister of Cnut the Great, whose son Harthacnut died without issue in 1042. According to the eleventh-century Uppland rune stones, women could also inherit land from children who died without descendants, and in some places women may have inherited a share of their parents' wealth, although the shares of sisters and brothers were not equal, notably because daughters had to be provided with dowries on marriage.

As we might expect, Viking children were taught from an early age to be tough and self-reliant. If a child was unwanted, he or she usually was left exposed to the elements and allowed to die. Although this practice was eventually banned due to the Christian influence, deformed children still were disposed of in this way. In common with so many other cultures, Viking children had their toys, games, and rhymes; but they were quickly educated in the importance of contributing to the running of their society, and from an early age were assigned various tasks.

We know nothing about Viking beliefs regarding the fate of children after death: there are no rune stones in memory of children, and they were not buried in adult cemeteries until the conversion to Christianity.

Clothes and Jewelry

There are a number of methods by which we can form a picture of what Vikings actually looked like and how they dressed. For a general impression we can turn to the words of the anthropologist Berit Sellevold, describing a typical Viking (quoted in Else Roesdahl):

> Both men and women were of harmonious proportions. The craniums are of medium width and medium height in relation to their length, and the faces are of medium height in relation to their width. Similarly, the eye-sockets and noses are of medium height in relation to their width. On average the left thigh-bone and shin-bone are a little longer than the right (which is also quite normal today). There is a slight difference between the sexes in the length of the arms: men's right upper arm is a little longer than the left, while women's upper arms are of almost equal length. This may be due to men using their right arms more than their left, while women used both arms almost equally. . . . In general appearance, Viking Age people were hardly any different to the Scandinavian population today — apart from slightly smaller stature and considerably better teeth, as well as dress, hair styles and jewelry, of course.

The popular image of the Viking as a filthy, unkempt barbarian with matted beard and hair flying is quite erroneous, at least with regard to the daily life of the Scandinavian people. From the very few naturalistic pictorial representations we have, we can see that Vikings were actually well groomed, with long and neatly plaited mustaches, and beards that did not extend upward to the cheeks. This is further supported by the discovery of various toilet articles, including combs, nail cleaners, tweezers, washing bowls, and even toothpicks. There also is evidence, in the form of a record left by a Spanish Arab named At-Tartūshi, who visited the town of Hedeby in the tenth century, that both men and women wore eye makeup. According to the English chronicler John of Wallingford, Vikings also bathed once a week, which accounted for their success with the opposite sex.

Of course, this salubrious picture cannot be applied to all Vikings: slaves and very poor peasants would doubtless have been much more wretched characters, their bodies bearing the signs of heavy labor and an inferior diet. Likewise, Vikings on long voyages doubtless let themselves slide somewhat. An Arab emissary named Ibn Fadhlan, who met a group of Vikings by the Volga in the early tenth century, was quite disgusted by them. He noted that they did not wash after defecating and urinating, nor after sexual intercourse or eating — all of which was of the utmost importance to a devout Muslim.

Viking women were highly skilled at clothmaking, taking raw flax or wool and spinning, dyeing, and bleaching it, weaving it into fine cloth and then cutting and sewing it into elegant garments. Using bone or bronze needles, they could take a ball of yarn and fashion socks and gloves, and spin fine silk threads into decorative braids. Although no complete items of Viking clothing have survived, many examples of shoes and boots have been discovered. The uppers usually were made of goatskin, and were fastened with a strap. Garments usually were made of wool, and sometimes of linen, with many different types of fur being used for trimming cloaks.

Concerning types of dress, Else Roesdahl writes in *The Vikings:*

Knitting was probably not known but warm garments were made of needle-binding (interlocking loops of yarn "sewn" together), as seen in a sock from Coppergate, York, and there were elegant "spranged" textiles (a kind of loose plaiting). Besides being trimmed with fur or imitation fur, clothes might be decorated with appliqué, embroidery, metal-wire decoration, plaited borders or tablet-woven bands which might contain gold or silver threads. They were often dyed in a range of colours. Heaps of walnut shells found in Hedeby were probably imported as a source of brown dye rather than because of a partiality for walnuts.

Viking men frequently wore narrow, ankle-length trousers, midcalf-length trousers similar to bell-bottoms, and plus-four-type trousers that probably were tied below the knee. They wore wool or linen undershirts and tunics that could either be tied or worn loose. On top of these they wore heavy cloaks, which were fastened with a large brooch at the right shoulder. Women usually wore a tight-fitting garment reaching to the ankles, with a shawl or cloak fastened at the front with a decorative brooch.

Although the Vikings were as fond of splendor and conspicuous displays of wealth as anyone, their jewelry was by and large functional. However, they were extremely fond of armrings, neckrings, and necklaces. They rarely wore finger rings and never earrings, which were characteristically Slav. Vikings tended to display their wealth in the form of armrings and neckrings; most of those that have been found in Scandinavia are of silver, and many of those were fashioned from melted Arabic silver coins.

Since Vikings carried their wealth with them in the form of jewelry, these items were made in standard weights. Payments usually were made in silver, so pieces of jewelry served as currency, and were cut into pieces if smaller sums were required.

Gold also was a popular choice for ornamentation. Else Roesdahl informs us that the largest piece of gold jewelry dating from the Viking Age is a neckring that was caught in the wheel of a seeder near Lake Tissø on the island of Sjælland, Denmark, in 1977. The ring is plaited from four thick bands. Roesdahl speculates that it was intended either for an idol, or for a wearer with a very broad chest.

The Vikings were very fond of brooches, and those discovered often display Scandinavian versions of foreign designs. The largest examples were given as gifts, and were not intended to be worn. (In *The Prose Edda,* Snorri Sturluson writes of one weighing twenty-five pounds, awarded by the Icelandic people to a poet who had written a particularly fine national poem).

The Vikings' Food and Home

Excavations of Viking settlements have revealed a great deal of information on what they ate. Meat figured prominently in their diet, including pork, beef, mutton, hens, and ducks. The usual method of preparation was to boil the meat with herbs and root vegetables. They also cooked their meat on spits and in skillets.

One of the most important crops was barley, from which the Vikings produced flour and malt to make bread, *grautr* (a kind of porridge), and ale. Rye, oats, and, in the southern regions of Scandinavia, wheat also were cultivated, as were beans, peas, turnips, and cabbage. Many types of fruit were gathered or cultivated, including small apples, plums, cherries, pears, blackberries, and elderberries, along with almonds, walnuts, hazelnuts, and chestnuts.

Fishing also was a very important activity, and a wide variety of fish were eaten, including herring, salmon, eel, pike, and roach, and also shellfish such as oysters, cockles, and mussels. Fish often was eaten fresh, but during less plentiful periods, it also was preserved by salting, pickling, or smoking. There is an interesting passage in the Colloquy of Aelfric, abbot of Eynsham, in which a fisherman explains his craft. He begins by boarding his boat and casting his net into the river, followed by a hook, bait, and basket. He sells his fish to the people of nearby towns, who eagerly buy his eels, pike, minnows, turbot, trout, and lampreys. Sometimes he fishes in the sea, but not often, as it takes a lot of rowing to get there. When he does fish in the sea, he catches herring, salmon, porpoises, sturgeon, crabs, flounder, and lobster, among many other things. When asked why he does not catch whales, the fisherman replies that it is very risky to go after whales, and it is far preferable to catch a small fish that can easily be killed than to chase a large animal that can kill one with a single stroke.

In common with most farming societies, the Vikings used their animals for more than just food: sheep were raised for their wool, and cows for their milk and hides. The horns of bulls were used as drinking vessels as well as for fastenings. Bones were fashioned into belt ends, needles, knife handles, and hairpins. Hens, ducks, and geese provided eggs as well as meat, and their hollow bones often were made into musical instruments.

Another important foodstuff was honey, the only sweetener available at the time, which was used as an ingredient in almond cakes, gingerbread, and dishes similar to cheesecake. Milk from cows, sheep, and goats was used to make butter and cheese. People ate with their fingers and a knife, and drank soup directly from a bowl or beaker. Although forks were not used, pointed "food sticks" have been found. Made from wood or bone, they seem to have been used to pierce and pick up pieces of meat and larger vegetables. Sometimes wooden plates were used, and beer and wine were drunk from wooden or pottery cups and mugs as well as from finely decorated drinking horns.

The Scandinavians were extremely fond of feasting. A royal feast would have been a lavish and rollicking affair. It took place in a long hall with benches along the walls. The king or chieftain occupied a special place in the center of one wall, while the other guests were seated according to their rank. All along the walls hung tapestries depicting scenes from the lives and exploits of gods and heroes. The room was lit by flickering oil lamps, while a fire roared in the hearth at the center of the hall.

The feast consisted of many kinds of meat and fish, boiled in cauldrons or roasted on great spits, and accompanied by bread, vegetables, fruits, and nuts. Of course, the food would be washed down with copious amounts of beer, wine, and mead, while the guests listened to the recitations of scalds (court poets) and the music of flutes and lyres. They might also be entertained by acrobats and jugglers. Such a feast might well last for several days, during which the guests took advantage of the pleasant surroundings to make or break friendships, take care of personal business, or arrange marriages.

The homestead was the center of Viking life, and the size and construction of houses depended very much both on the materials available and the social standing of the owners. The houses of the nobility were characterized by size and quality of construction and probably were elaborately decorated with fine carvings and vibrant colors. A good example of the typical Viking town house was excavated at Hedeby, an important trading center in Jutland. Dendrochronology has demonstrated that the house was built in the year 870, at the height of the Viking expeditions overseas. A full-size replica of this house was built at Moesgård Museum in Denmark.

The Hedeby house measured 39 feet long by 16 feet wide, with wattle and daub walls built around a timber frame. The weight of the roof was distributed evenly over seven sloping outer posts attached to the long walls. The interior space was divided into three rooms. The central room was dominated by a large central hearth, and there were wide platforms against the walls. This room functioned as both kitchen and living room. There was a gable room on each side of the central room, the larger containing a domed baking oven, and the smaller serving as either workshop or storage area.

Both the main house and its outbuildings were secured with locks made either of iron or wood, and theft from locked areas was considered an extremely serious crime. The mistress of the house looked after the keys; this responsibility was taken very seriously, and conferred status on the key-bearer.

The house's interior would have been steeped in perpetual semidarkness, as the windows were few and very small. The only significant light would have come from the hearth, the shutters in the roof that allowed smoke to escape, and the oil lamps and tallow candles by which the women sewed or wove. As with dwellings throughout the world, the hearth was the focal point of the main living room, and was used for both heat and cooking. Since there was no chimney, and the roof shutters cannot have been particularly efficient as extractors, the house was often very smoky. Else Roesdahl notes that "many people must have suffered from slight carbon-dioxide poisoning, especially in winter when they had to spend much time indoors."

The stamped-earth floor was covered with hay or straw and was bounded on each side by a low platform of earth, usually about 3.3 to 5 feet deep. It was on these platforms that the house's inhabitants spent most of their time: they were living spaces, as opposed to the floor, which was used only for walking on.

Furnishings included rugs, tapestries, cushions, and storage items such as caskets and chests. Although there probably were low stools, Scandinavians usually sat cross-legged on the living room's raised platforms. The house did not include separate bedrooms: people either slept in small alcoves, or on the raised platforms on rugs that were rolled out for the night. Much of the space in the house would almost certainly have been taken up by provisions.

In *The Vikings*, Else Roesdahl refers to scaldic poems and graves in describing the furnishings of wealthy households:

An enormous quantity of fine items was buried with the woman in the Oseberg mound in southern Norway in the year 834. Most of the grave-goods were of wood, often lavishly carved and sometimes decorated with paintings and metal fittings, but there were also textiles and metal objects. These furnishings, kitchen utensils, tools for many kinds of textile work, vehicles (a ship, a wagon and sledges), farm-tools, etc., came from a king's or chieftain's house. There was a narrow frieze of a tapestry decorated with narrative scenes, a chair, many chests, at least five beds (perhaps specially built for travelling, as they can be easily taken apart), bedding stuffed with feathers and down, tall oil lamps, looms, finely wrought hooks for hanging cauldrons, cauldrons, griddles, buckets, barrels, tubs, troughs, scoops, knives, ladles and much else including food.

Money

Viking trading and raiding brought truly colossal amounts of silver and gold to Scandinavia. During the ninth century, the Frankish rulers surrendered more than 44,000 pounds of silver to the Vikings (there must have been many more payments that were not included in the written sources), and this does not take account of the additional goods and precious metals that the Vikings stole from the poorly defended communities of eastern and western Europe. Between the years 991 and 1014, the Vikings received more than 150,000 pounds of silver in danegeld payments from England, "the equivalent of at least 36 million contemporary coins," according to Else Roesdahl.

In addition to the information given in the written records from the period, numerous hoards from the Viking Age have been discovered (a hoard is defined as two or more objects made of precious metal and deliberately buried in the ground). Hoards normally include coins, jewelry, ingots, and other precious objects. The largest Viking hoard so far discovered is from Cuerdale in England and contained 88 pounds of silver.

We can determine the origin of Scandinavian silver by means

of the inscriptions on the coins, which tell when and where they were minted. A huge number — more than two hundred thousand — have been discovered in Scandinavia, mainly in Sweden. According to Roesdahl:

> Coins until c. 970 are predominantly Arabic; more than 85,000 have been found in Scandinavia. Many were minted in the eastern parts of the Caliphate, in what is now Samarkand and Tashkent. It is worth remembering that the vast numbers that fell into the hands of the Vikings represent only a small percentage of the silver of the Orient. After 970 the Scandinavians had to turn to Western Europe for silver, as the Eastern supply routes began to dry up rapidly. The exploitation of German silver mines in the Harz Mountains increased at this time, and of the German coins that ended up in Scandinavia about 70,000 have been found. In addition there are more than 40,000 Anglo-Saxon coins from the second half of the tenth and the eleventh centuries, more than have been found in England itself. A fair number of these no doubt came from the large payments of Danegeld.

The cutting up of jewelry to make up the remainder of a certain price (referred to earlier) was particularly common in Denmark and Skåne between the tenth and eleventh centuries. This practice was not followed in northern Norway, where barter still was the common form of trade. There were many large hoards on Gotland, and it is believed that these constituted profits made through trading with Russia, or perhaps were gains from plunder. There are a number of possible reasons for hoarding coins and other valuables: there may have been disturbances in the region that may have made it potentially dangerous to have one's wealth in plain view; the owners may have decided to leave their homes for some reason and were reluctant to take their valuables with them; or perhaps it was simply the custom to bury one's valuables close by, as on Gotland.

Denmark was the first of the Scandinavian countries to mint coins, which were used as currency at the trading center of Ribe in the eighth century. Less than a century later, a mint was established at Hedeby, and coin production continued during the reigns of Svein Fork-Beard and Harald Sveinsson.

Slaves and the Free

Although slavery played an important part in Viking society, we know very little about their slaves. This is only to be expected, since by definition they had no influence on political and economic life. The popular image of Viking marauders carrying off men and women to be kept or sold as slaves is doubtless accurate, and this was the purpose of many Viking expeditions. Once captured, the slaves might be kept, sold to others, or if the captives came from rich families, held for ransom. Christian captives sometimes were freed after a ransom had been paid by the church.

Such raids could come at any time, and without warning. According to the annals of the monastery of Xanten on the Rhine, such a raid happened in 837. Following the appearance of Halley's Comet (never a good sign), the Vikings laid waste the island of Walcheren at the mouth of the Schelde River in southern Holland and carried off many women as well as many goods and valuables.

Without doubt, slaves could expect a very hard life; however, there were a number of rules governing their treatment. They were put to work in houses and as agricultural laborers in the fields, as well as on various construction projects. Although many women were used for sexual gratification, if a woman was particularly beautiful or accomplished in some art or craft, she could expect to be treated with much greater respect and could live in relatively comfortable conditions. However, a slave who misbehaved or ran away could expect no mercy. If he committed a crime, he could not be fined, since he possessed nothing. The answer was as simple as it was brutal: he would be beaten, maimed for life, or even killed. The runaway was hunted down like a wild animal, and when cornered suffered the wild animal's fate beneath a lethal rain of blows.

On the whole, slaves were considered with some distaste in Viking society, and this is illustrated in one of the Eddas, the poem "RígsÞula," which concerns the god Heimdall (called Ríg in the poem). As Else Roesdahl notes, the poem describes the three distinct social classes into which Viking society was divided: slaves, the free, and the ruling elite. The poem, which is generally though not unanimously considered to date from the tenth century, describes the origin of the three tiers of Scandinavian society. While on a journey, Ríg came upon a hut in which lived a poor couple called Ai and Edda (Great-Grandfather and Great-Grandmother, respectively). They gave him coarse bread to eat and allowed him to share their bed. Following this visit, the couple had a son whom they called Þræl (Thrall or Slave). Although the son thrived, the poem paints a rather grim physical portrait: "[O]n his hand was wrinkled skin, gnarled knuckles, thick fingers, foul the face, long the heels." He married a girl named Þír (also Slave), who was not much better: "[D]irt was on her sole, her arm sunburnt, crooked her nose." They had many children, all of whom were condemned to lives of ugliness and drudgery. The boys were called Noisy, Byreboy, Roughneck, and Horsefly, and the girls Lazybones, Beanpole, and Fatty. From this family descended the race of slaves.

Ríg next stayed with a couple who were altogether more prosperous and who lived in a hall. They were called Afi and Amma (Grandfather and Grandmother, respectively). Once again, Ríg shared their bed, lying between them. When they had a son they named him Karl (meaning farmer, or free man). He was healthy and had twinkling eyes. "Ox he learnt to tame, plough to make, house to build and barn to raise, carts to make and turn the plough." He married a girl who came to his farm carrying keys, a symbol of feminine dignity. Her name was

Snör (Daughter-in-Law), and they had many healthy, attractive children. The boys were called Strongbeard, Husbandman, Holder, and Smith, and the girls Prettyface, Maiden, and Capable.

Finally, Ríg stayed with a rich couple who lived in a magnificent house. They were called Faðir and Móðir (Father and Mother, respectively). They presented Ríg with a splendid banquet of pork, game, white bread, and plenty of wine served in silver drinking bowls. Once again, he spent each night of his visit lying in bed between them. When their son was born, he was given the name Jarl (earl). Fair-haired and bright-cheeked, he became a fierce warrior, with much land to his name. His wife, Erna (Lively), was slender, wise, and exceptionally beautiful, and they had many children, the last of whom was called Konr ungr (King).

When a master died, sometimes his slaves would be killed so they might accompany him into the afterlife. When archaeologists excavated a tenth-century grave in Stengade, Langeland, Denmark, they discovered two skeletons. One of the skeletons had apparently had its feet tied together, and its skull lay at right angles to the rest of the bones, suggesting that it had been decapitated. Slaves who were not buried with their master or mistress (for women could be buried with slaves also) were simply placed in a hole in the ground.

Slavery was not necessarily for life: slaves could be freed by their owners, or eventually buy their own freedom if they were allowed to work for money. However, the newly freed slave still was a member of the landless class, and had little option but to seek employment as a farm laborer or servant.

In Viking society the free obviously included the aristocracy, but also a large number of professions, from landowners and tenant farmers to hunters and craftsmen, who together formed the economic backbone of the society. Although they varied considerably in their wealth and position, they had the right to express their views at the assembly (known as the Thing), where concerns of public interest were discussed.

They also enjoyed legal rights, attended religious and lay ceremonies, bore witness and produced verdicts, and contributed to society in various other ways, including making weapons, manning ships, and working in wood and metal.

The basic occupation was agriculture, with those possessing very large areas of land subdividing it into smaller tracts and leasing them out. Free men did not have to remain within the local community to achieve wealth: they could join an expedition to other lands, or even emigrate. In *The Vikings* Else Roesdahl cites Uppland in central Sweden as the best example of Viking internationalism. The region contains many rune stones, raised in the eleventh century, which tell of Viking journeys to lands throughout the known world:

> These rune stones were raised by self-satisfied, rich farmers, whom the Swedish historian Erik Lönnroth has dubbed "*nouveau-riche* upstarts." According to Lönnroth they needed to show off their wealth and fame, unlike the old aristocracy, who often buried their dead in family burial grounds in ships with rich furnishings (as at Vendel, Valsgärde and Tuna). Most of these *nouveau-riche* farmers were also Christians, like the king, but in contrast to the old aristocracy, and the king may well have made use of this ambitious stratum of society to strengthen his power in the area. In return, they may have been given administrative posts and special favours.

Runic inscriptions also tell us much about the rules of kinship the Vikings followed. For instance, a person's kin combined both the maternal and paternal families, and opportunities in life usually were decided by relationships within the immediate family. However, other factors also were important, such as the *félag* (fellowship), which could consist of a band of warriors, a trade association, or the owners of a ship. One rune stone from Århus in Jutland, again cited by Roesdahl, refers to a man named Asser Saxe, who seems to have been a member of a miltary fellowship as a warrior (or *dreng*), and also a part-owner of a ship. The rune stone was erected by his fellows and reads:

> Toste and Hove jointly with Frøbjørn erected this stone in memory of Asser Saxe, their partner, a very noble dreng. He died as the greatest "un-dastard" among men; he owned a ship together with Arne.

4

Journeys to a New World

These oak-hearted warriors
Lured me to this land
With promise of choice drinks;
Now I could curse this country!
For I, the helmet-wearer,
Must now grovel at a spring
And wield a water-pail;
No wine has touched my lips.

— *Eirik's Saga*

The Sagas

The first sagas were written early in the twelfth century and were intended as an addition to the "learned works" written under the auspices of the Icelandic Church. Their function was initially twofold: to provide serious popular entertainment with which to educate the people, and as a distraction from what the church considered to be undesirable forms of entertainment, such as dancing. The sagas concentrated on either individuals or communities. Most were anonymously written, although some (e.g., the *Heimskringla,* which chronicles the lives of Norwegian kings) were written by the Icelandic writer and historian Snorri Sturluson.

Medieval Iceland was a republic, without a royal court, which could serve as a cultural center, and around which historical and literary tradition could revolve. The people who had initially colonized the island were farmers and homesteaders, and as such were equal in social standing; and so when Ari the Learned came to write the first history of Iceland early in the twelfth century, he found himself describing the adventures and exploits not of a single ruling family but of all the families who had made the dangerous voyage to that harsh new land.

The writing of the sagas marked the beginning of the transition from the oral tradition to the literary, a process that was helped by the fact that at that time the origins of Icelandic society were still recent enough to be remembered without the aid of mythmaking and legendry. Nor had Iceland yet developed a rigid caste system by which the strata of society were demarcated. As the Icelandic historians and translators of sagas Magnus Magnusson and Hermann Pálsson note in *The Vinland Sagas:*

> Priests were farmers, aristocrats were priests, farmers were poets, and poets were peasants. Books were never the exclusive possession of any one class, nor was literacy. For instance, the school that was founded at Holar, in the north of Iceland, at the beginning of the twelfth century had a wide scatter of pupils, including women; and mention is specifically made of a church carpenter there, one Thorodd Gamlason, who became highly proficient in Latin. This policy of widespread general education meant that there was a large reservoir of literary capacity available for the conversion of oral material into written sagas.

For the first several hundred years of the Scandinavian settlement of Iceland, there were no villages: the inhabitants lived on farms, many of which were extremely isolated, and so not only did they have to be able to support themselves economically, but culturally also. This took the form of ballads to which the people danced, and also stories of the past and the latest news and gossip.

As previously noted, the church disapproved of dancing, and in a successful attempt to point the people in a more acceptable and intellectually profitable direction, it distributed books on various subjects, including the lives of saints. Although priests visited the many isolated parishes to read aloud from these books, they later encouraged the people to read from the books themselves. So enthusiastic was the people's response that the priests found themselves facing a growing demand for books. The first bishop of Holar responded in turn by engaging a number of copyists to transcribe new manuscripts, which were then distributed among the farms.

Although the first sagas were religious in theme, they quickly developed into secular stories, written expressly for entertainment. Magnusson and Pálsson offer as an example a wedding at Reykholar in 1119:

> On this celebrated occasion, which is described in the *Saga of Thorgils and Haflidi,* a priest called Ingimund Einarsson and a farmer called Hrolf of Skalmarness recited sagas which they themselves had "composed" — apparently for the purpose of entertaining the assembled wedding guests. One of these sagas still survives in a much later metrical version; it was about a legendary warrior-king called Hromund Gripsson. But the other, about Orm the Barra-Poet, is now, unfortunately, lost.

This chapter is based primarily on *Grænlendinga Saga* (Greenlanders' Saga), which was written in the late twelfth century, but also with reference to *Eirik's Saga,* which was written much later. These two sagas are the only sources that provide us with details of the Norse attempt to colonize the Atlantic coast of the North American continent.

Grœnlendinga Saga was intended primarily as entertainment, an exciting adventure story telling of the deeds of heroic Norse explorers; but it also was a work of history and geography, albeit a relatively unsophisticated one. Ironically, although *Eirik's Saga* was written much later, when saga writing had reached its greatest maturity of composition and expression, historians consider *Grœnlendinga Saga* to be the more trustworthy as a historical document. The earlier saga still should be treated with caution, however. In his book *The Vikings*, Magnus Magnusson writes:

> It now seems quite certain that *Eirik's Saga* was written as a conscious correction, improvement indeed, of the much earlier *Grœnlendinga Saga* in the light of what the author considered to be more reliable information. . . . The traditional view used to be that *Eirik's Saga* was the "better" of the two, from a literary standpoint, and therefore the earlier; but the problem of the relationship between the two sagas was brilliantly resolved by the Icelandic historian Professor Jón Jóhannesson. It was a stunning piece of literary detective work, which proved beyond any reasonable doubt that *Grœnlendinga Saga*, far from being later than *Eirik's Saga*, was in fact one of the earliest of all the Icelandic sagas, written only about 150 years after the time of the Vinland adventure.

The solution to the problem of dating the two sagas in relation to one another lay in the person of King Olaf Tryggvason of Norway, who was instrumental in the conversion of Iceland in the year 1000, and so was considered a champion of Christianity by the saga writers. However, medieval historians such as Saxo Grammaticus of Denmark and Adam of Bremen saw Olaf in an altogether less sympathetic light. "To them," writes Magnusson, "he was anathema: no evangelist, not even a Christian, more like Antichrist — a foreign usurper who seized the throne of Norway by force and wrought untold harm in that country before his unlamented death in battle in 1000."

In about the year 1200, an Icelandic monk named Odd Snorrason wrote a biography of King Olaf in which he claimed that the king also had converted Greenland to Christianity. Professor Jóhannesson noted that the *Grænlendinga Saga* does not mention King Olaf in relation to the Greenland conversion and so must have been written before Odd Snorrason invented the story.

Although neither saga can be said to be a completely accurate historical record, there is no doubt that the Vikings did discover North America five hundred years before Columbus. In 1961, the Norwegian archaeologists Helge Ingstad and his wife, Anne Stine Ingstad, discovered a Viking settlement on the Newfoundland coast at Epaves Bay called L'anse aux Meadows (Meadow Cove). This is the only Viking settlement on the North American continent that is considered genuine, although, as we shall see at the end of this chapter, there have been numerous other — albeit spurious — claims for a Viking presence much farther inland. The Ingstads' excavations revealed the outlines of eight sod-walled structures, one of which had apparently been a bathhouse similar to those found in Viking settlements in Greenland. They also found iron nail fragments, pieces of iron slag from a blacksmith's workshop, a soapstone spindle whorl, and a bronze pin.

This tiny cluster of houses could have accommodated no more than about ninety people, and it was occupied for only a few years between 1000 and 1020, according to radiocarbon dating from various parts of the site. It is likely that L'anse aux Meadows served as a base from which to launch exploratory expeditions farther south, since butternuts (which do not grow north of the St. Lawrence River) have been found there. There is no evidence that it was a farming community: the inhabitants seem to have devoted themselves largely to exploration and ship repair, and supported themselves by hunting and fishing.

Eirik the Red Leaves Iceland

Late in the tenth century, Eirik the Red and his father, Thorvald, left their home in Jaederen, Norway. Thorvald had been exiled for manslaughter, and sailed with his son for Iceland, which had by that time been extensively settled. They made their home at Drangar, and when Thorvald died, Eirik married a woman named Thjodhild. They moved south, to Eirikstead, near Vatnshorn, and had a son they named Leif, who would become as famous as his father.

Eirik was as quick-tempered as Thorvald had been. When his slaves accidentally started a landslide that destroyed the farm of a man named Valthjof, one of Valthjof's kinsmen, Eyjolf Saur, killed them. Eirik then took his revenge and killed both Eyjolf Saur and another man, named Hrafn the Dueler. Eyjolf's kinsmen took action in turn to avenge the deaths, and Eirik was banished from his home. Unable to return to Norway because of his father's crime, he decided to move to Brok Island and Oxen Island.

At about this time he lent a set of household bench boards to a man named Thorgest of Breidabolstead. When he asked for the bench boards back, Thorgest refused, and this was the catalyst for yet more violent trouble. Eirik went to Breidabolstead to retrieve his property. A fight ensued and several men were killed, including two of Thorgest's sons.

It was plain that Eirik was what we would today call a "loose cannon." The local assembly passed a three-year sentence of full outlawry, which required him to leave Iceland for three years on pain of summary execution. With Thorgest and his men searching high and low for him so that they might dispense their own form of justice, Eirik made his ship ready and set sail for a new land that was rumored to lie to the west. Sailing past Snæfells Glacier, he disappeared over the horizon and eventually made landfall at the place he was seeking, near a glacier he named Mid-Glacier. The course he had taken between the two gigantic glaciers became the regular sailing route between Iceland and Greenland until the fourteenth century.

Eirik then sailed south down the coast, to see whether there were any habitable regions in the new land. In 981 or 982, after rounding the southernmost point, which came to be known as Cape Farewell, he proceeded up the western coastline until he came to an island at the mouth of a great fjord. He spent his first winter on this island, and in the spring entered the fjord and decided to make his home there. When summer came, Eirik began to explore the surrounding regions, and gave names to many of the places he discovered.

After spending the next two summers exploring the icy fastnesses of the new land, Eirik returned to Iceland. He named the western realm Greenland, believing that people would be more willing to travel there if it had a pleasant name. In fact, the coast of the great island was indeed green, due to the slightly warmer climate the Far North was enjoying at that time. Eirik spent the winter in Iceland and then set sail west once again; this time his intention was colonization.

According to the twelfth-century historians of Iceland, in the early summer of 985 or 986, Eirik the Red set off with twenty-five ships, which sailed from Breidafjord and Borgarfjord. Only fourteen reached their destination: some were driven back by the dreadful force of the elements, and some were lost entirely.

When the remainder finally arrived, they discovered artifacts that proved there had once been other people there. In his *Íslendingabók*, written in about 1130, the historian Ari the Learned wrote:

Both to the east and west of the country they found human habitations, and the remains of skin-boats, and stone artifacts, from which it can be concluded that the people who had been there before were of the same race as those who inhabited Vinland, whom the Greenlanders call Skrælings.

The Vikings had discovered belongings of the Inuit natives of Greenland. As Magnus Magnusson states, it was quite reasonable for Ari the Learned to identify the native Greenlanders with the Native Americans the Vikings were later to meet in Vinland, "based on an observed similarity between two Stone Age material cultures." The word "Skræling" is difficult to translate, but it is certainly contemptuous, and means something like "wretch" or "savage."

Eirik made his home at Brattahlid in southern Greenland, and enjoyed the respect and admiration of the others who had accompanied him. He had three sons — Leif, Thorvald, and Thorstein — and a daughter named Freydis, who lived with her husband, Thorvard, at Gardar. At this time, Brattahlid in the Eastern Settlement formed the nucleus of the Viking colony.

Bjarni's Voyage

In about the year 985, a young man named Bjarni arrived in Eyrar, Iceland, intending to spend the winter with his father, Herjolf Bardarson, as was his habit. Bjarni was a brave and enterprising youth, and had earned wealth and an enviable reputation during his voyages to foreign lands. However, on this occasion, when he arrived at Eyrar, he was given the shocking news that in his absence his father had sold the family farm and immigrated to Greenland with Eirik the Red. When Bjarni's crew asked him what he intended to do, he replied that he aimed to preserve his family's tradition and spend the winter with his father. "I will sail to Greenland," he declared, "if you are willing to come with me."

His crew replied that they were willing to do whatever he thought best. Bjarni warned them that many would consider the voyage inadvisable, since none of them had ever sailed the Greenland Sea. This did not deter Bjarni's stout crew, so they immediately set sail.

For the first three days, conditions were good; but then

the bitter winds of the North assailed them, and a thick fog descended. Before long they had no idea what their course was. The gods were kind to them, however, for presently the fog lifted, revealing the sun, and after just one more day's sailing, they sighted land. The crew discussed whether this was really the land they were seeking. Bjarni said he doubted that it was Greenland, and was proved correct when they sailed closer and discovered that the land was not mountainous, but rather hilly and wooded.

They set sail again, and after another two days sighted land once more. But this could not be Greenland either. Bjarni declared that Greenland was flanked by mighty glaciers, and this place was flat and wooded. So once again they put out to sea, and spied nothing but powerful, roiling waves for the next three days.

They sighted land for a third time, and noted with glad hearts that it was high and mountainous; and in the distance they could make out a titanic glacier. The crew turned to their leader and asked him if he intended to land here; but Bjarni replied that he considered this place worthless. As they followed the coastline, they saw that Bjarni was correct: this was a small island.

As they set out once again, a mighty gale blew up, threatening to destroy the ship's sail and rigging. For another four days the crew battled the elements, not knowing whether their ship would last in the face of this onslaught. When they sighted a fourth land, the crew asked Bjarni if he thought that this, at last, might be their intended destination. To their relief, Bjarni declared that this land fitted most closely the descriptions he had heard of Greenland, so here they would land.

They went ashore at dusk on a promontory on which another boat had been brought to rest. This boat, they later discovered, belonged to Bjarni's father, Herjolf. Bjarni decided to give up trading, and stayed with his father at the place, which was later named Herjolfsness. Bjarni continued to farm there after his father's death.

Sometime later, Bjarni sailed to Norway to visit Earl Eirik Hakonarson, who ruled Norway from 1000 to 1014. Earl Eirik made his visitor very welcome, and listened with great interest to his tales of the lands he had explored to the west. Bjarni returned to his home in Greenland the following summer, having been made a retainer at Earl Eirik's court.

Leif Eiriksson's Voyage

In about the year 985, Bjarni Herjolfsson had been blown off course from Greenland and had briefly sighted land to the west. Fifteen years later, Leif, a son of Eirik the Red, visited Bjarni and bought his ship from him. After engaging a crew of thirty-five, Leif asked his father if he would agree to accompany them in their attempt to investigate Bjarni's sighting. Eirik replied that he was getting old and could not endure the hardships of long voyages as well as he used to. Leif replied that he retained his great luck, and eventually persuaded his father to go with them.

However, as he was riding toward the ship, Eirik's horse stumbled and he was thrown, injuring his leg. The Vikings considered a fall from a horse a very bad omen, and Eirik took this as a sign that he was not destined to discover any more lands. He returned to Brattahlid, and Leif set sail from Greenland's Eastern Settlement into the unknown.

Heading northwest, he first sighted a bleak land of rock and glaciers. Although this place did not at all seem promising, they cast anchor and made landfall in a small boat. Leif said to his companions: "We have done better than Bjarni where this country is concerned — we at least have set foot on it. I shall give this country a name and call it Helluland." This name literally meant Slab Land, since the area of land between the glaciers and the shore was like a single great slab of gray rock.

They put out to sea, heading south, and presently sighted a second land. Once again they made landfall in a small boat, and found themselves in a country that was flat and wooded.

Leif declared that he would name this land after its resources, and called it Markland (Forest Land).

Once again the crew headed off onto the sea, still following a southerly course. Two days later, they sighted land again. This land had a milder climate, and its rivers were filled with salmon. The Vikings ran their hands across the dew-covered grass and put the dew to their lips, savoring its sweetness.

Leif and his crew decided to spend the winter there, and built some large houses for themselves. When this job had been done, Leif said to his companions: "I shall divide our company into two parties and explore this country. Half of the company shall remain here at the houses, while the other half go exploring. But they must not go so far that they cannot return the same evening, and they are not to become separated."

For some time they carried out these instructions, with Leif himself alternately going out with the exploring party and remaining behind at their camp. One evening the Vikings discovered that one of their number was missing. It was Tyrkir the Southerner (in other words, a German). Tyrkir and Leif were old and dear friends who had been devoted to each other since childhood, and Leif was extremely angry when told that Tyrkir was nowhere to be found. Immediately Leif chose twelve men to accompany him on a search for the missing man.

They had walked only a short distance when Tyrkir came out of the trees toward them. After welcoming him back, Leif asked him how he had become separated from the rest of the group. Tyrkir replied: "I did not go much farther than you. I have some news: I found vines and grapes."

The following morning Leif said to his men: "Now we have two tasks on our hands. On alternate days we must gather grapes and cut vines, and then fell trees, to make cargo for my ship." This would be a valuable cargo indeed, since there were no trees in Greenland, and timber had to be imported.

They took on a full cargo of timber, and in the spring sailed away from the new land, which Leif decided to call Vinland (Wine Land), after the copious wild grapes found there.

It is impossible to be absolutely certain as to the locations of Leif's discoveries. We can say with some confidence that Helluland was Baffin Island, and Markland was Labrador. However, the location of Vinland is more difficult to ascertain. The only known Viking settlement on the North American continent is at L'Anse aux Meadows in Newfoundland, but this is too far north to correspond satisfactorily with the descriptions of Vinland preserved in the sagas. It is more likely that Vinland lay south of the Gulf of St. Lawrence in what is now Nova Scotia, which is the only area containing both wild grapes and Atlantic salmon.

As Leif and his crew were nearing Greenland, he caught sight of something strange in the distance — something that might have been a reef, or perhaps a ship. Leif had the keenest eyesight, and soon was able to make out the figures of several people standing on what he realized was a reef.

Turning to the others, he said: "I want to sail close into the wind to reach these people. If they need our help, it is our duty to give it; but if they are hostile, then the advantages are all on our side and none on theirs."

They anchored just off the reef and put out a boat to meet the people standing on it. The leader, who was from Norway, told them his name: Thorir. When Leif introduced himself, Thorir replied: "Are you a son of Eirik the Red of Brattahlid?"

Leif replied that he was, and invited the others aboard his ship with as many of their belongings as the vessel could carry. In all, he rescued fifteen people from the reef, and from then on he was known as Leif the Lucky. News of Leif's voyage to Vinland spread rapidly, and his brother Thorvald decided to sail there to explore it further. Leif told his brother that he would give him his own ship to make the journey.

Thorvald's Voyage

With his brother's help and guidance, Thorvald prepared his expedition and recruited a crew of thirty. There are no records of his voyage to Vinland until his arrival at Leif's camp, where the new explorers spent the winter.

When spring arrived, Thorvald decided to send a small number of men to sail west along the coast in the ship's boat, and explore that region. The country there was beautiful, with sandy beaches and gentle, wood-covered hills. As they explored the land and the numerous islands all around, they made a curious discovery: a wooden stack cover, which indicated that there were other people here, although no one was in sight.

The following summer, Thorvald took his ship east and then north along the coast, where they encountered a fierce gale that drove the ship onto the shore, shattering its keel. It took them a long time to repair the keel, and when they had done so, Thorvald erected the old keel on the headland on which they had been driven, and called the place Kjalarness (Keel Ness).

Their ship repaired, the Vikings continued eastward until they found themselves facing a promontory separating the mouths of two fjords. The promontory was heavily wooded, and Thorvald remarked on its great beauty, adding that he would very much like to make his home there.

On their way back to the ship, they came upon more evidence of human presence: three humps that lay on the beach. They approached carefully and saw that the objects were boats made of animal skin. Beneath each of the boats lay three sleeping men. The Vikings fell on them and killed them all except one, who managed to escape in his boat. Thorvald surveyed the country surrounding the headland and spied a number of other humps in the distance, which he assumed were settlements. It is possible that these settlements belonged to the Micmac, or now-extinct Beothuk tribes.

The Vikings had grown weary and fatigued, and lay down to sleep for a while. They were suddenly jolted awake by one of their number, who shouted for them to get back to their ship as quickly as possible. Thorvald glanced around and saw a swarm of boats coming toward them. He ordered his men to assume defensive positions along the gunwales of their ship. The Skrælings shot arrows at them for a while, then rapidly withdrew.

Thorvald was the only one wounded. "An arrow flew up between the gunwale and my shield," he said, "under my arm — here it is. This will lead to my death." He continued: "I advise you to return as soon as you can. But first I want you to take me to the headland I thought so suitable for a home. I seem to have hit on the truth when I said that I would settle there for a while. Bury me there and put crosses at my head and feet, and let the place be called Krossaness (Cross Ness) for ever afterward."

Thorvald died, and his men carried out his wishes, for Greenland had been converted to Christianity in the year 1000. They then sailed back to join the rest of the expedition, telling their comrades the sad news. They spent the winter gathering grapes and vines to take back to Greenland, and set sail the following spring.

The Death of Thorstein Eiriksson

When he received the news of his brother's death in Vinland, Thorstein Eiriksson determined to set sail immediately so he might retrieve his body and bring it home to Greenland. He crewed Thorvald's ship with twenty-five of the strongest men he could find, and took his wife, Gudrid, as well.

Luck was not on their side, however, and as soon as they were out of sight of land, the elements descended on them so that they lost all track of where they were going. Eventually they made land at Lysufjord, in the Western Settlement of Greenland. Thorstein found lodgings for his crew but could find none for himself and Gudrid, and so they stayed on the ship.

A few days later, a man named Thorstein the Black came to the ship and offered to put up Thorstein and Gudrid in his home. When they accepted the invitation, Thorstein the Black said: "Then I shall be back tomorrow with a cart to fetch you. There is no lack of means to provide for you, but you will find life at my house very dull, for there are only the two of us, my wife and myself, and I am very unsociable."

In spite of this less-than-welcoming statement, Thorstein the Black was true to his word. The following morning he returned with a cart and took them to his house, where they were very well looked after.

This was but a brief respite in Thorstein Eiriksson's fortunes, for that winter brought with it a disease that killed most of his crew before spreading to the house of Thorstein the Black. The first to fall ill was his wife, Grimhild, a giant of a woman whose great physical strength could not protect her. As the disease forced Grimhild to her bed, Thorstein Eiriksson also caught it.

Apparently Grimhild died, and her husband went outside to find a wooden board on which to lay her body. While he was gone, Grimhild raised herself on one elbow, put her feet out of the bed, and began to look for her shoes. When her husband returned to the room, she fell back on the bed with such force that the whole house shook. Thorstein the Black made a coffin for his wife and took her away for burial.

Thorstein Eiriksson finally succumbed to the disease and he, too, apparently died. Thorstein the Black attempted to console the distraught Gudrid, telling her that he would see to it that she, her husband, and his dead crew would be returned to Eiriksfjord. As she thanked their host, her husband suddenly sat up in bed and said, "Where is Gudrid?"

Gudrid glanced at Thorstein the Black and said, "Should I answer him?"

Thorstein the Black shook his head and approached his guest, saying, "What is it you want?"

Thorstein Eiriksson replied, "I wish to tell Gudrid her destiny, so that she may resign herself better to my death, for I am now in a happy place of repose. I have this to say to you, Gudrid: You will marry an Icelander and you will have a long life together and your children shall be great and vigorous, bright and excellent, sweet and fragrant. You and your husband will go from Greenland to Norway, and from there to Iceland, where you will make your home and live for a long time. You will survive your husband and go on a pilgrimage to Rome, then return to your farm in Iceland; a church will be built there and you will be ordained a nun and stay there until you die."

Thorstein Eiriksson then fell back on his bed and died, and his body was taken to his ship. Thorstein the Black made good on his promise: He sold his farm and livestock, engaged a crew, and took Gudrid, her husband, and their crew back to Eiriksfjord. Gudrid went to stay with her brother-in-law Leif Eiriksson at Brattahlid, while Thorstein the Black made his home in Eiriksfjord, where he remained for the rest of his life.

Karlsefni Fights the Skrælings

The following summer, a ship arrived from Norway. Her captain, Thorfinn Karlsefni, was extremely wealthy. He spent the winter with Leif Eiriksson at Brattahlid and fell in love with Gudrid. They were married that same winter.

Vinland still was the subject of much conversation, and everyone, including Gudrid, urged Karlsefni to make the journey. He eventually agreed, and brought together a crew of sixty men, five women (including Gudrid), and all manner of livestock. The company agreed to share equally any profits arising from the voyage, and, if possible, to establish a permanent colony there.

They reached Vinland without incident, found Leif Eiriksson's houses, and put their beasts out to graze. Karlsefni ordered his men to begin felling timber, which they would then cut into lengths and leave out to season before loading it onto the ship.

The following summer, the Viking explorers had their first encounter with the Skrælings, who came out of the woods one day and approached the grazing animals. The bull began to bellow in fear and anger, and the startled Skrælings ran to the houses and tried to get inside, but Karlsefni ordered the doors barred against them. Although neither group could understand each other's language, a first fumbling attempt at trade was made between them. The Skrælings offered the contents of their packs — furs and pelts — in return for weapons. Karlsefni refused to sell any arms, and told the women to take out some milk. When the Skrælings saw the milk, they gladly agreed to trade their pelts for it, and went away satisfied.

Karlsefni did not want to take any chances with his colony's safety, and ordered his men to build a wooden palisade around the houses. At about this time he and Gudrid had a son, whom they named Snorri.

The following winter, the Skrælings returned, wishing to trade more pelts for the Vikings' milk, and once again they went away satisfied.

One day a curious thing happened. Gudrid was sitting in the doorway of a house, with Snorri in his cradle beside her, when a woman with pale skin and chestnut hair approached. When she looked up, Gudrid found herself gazing into the largest eyes she had ever seen in a human. The woman was short, dressed in a close-fitting tunic, and wore a band around her hair.

"What is your name?" asked the strange woman.

"My name is Gudrid. What is yours?"

"My name is Gudrid," came the reply.

Just as Gudrid invited the stranger to sit beside her, she heard a loud crash, and the stranger vanished. At the same moment, one of the Vikings killed a Skræling who was trying to steal some weapons. The other Skrælings immediately fled.

Karlsefni called a meeting, and told the others that they needed to come up with a plan to defend themselves, for the Skrælings were sure to return with intentions other than trade. He continued: "Ten men are to go out on the headland and make themselves conspicuous, and the rest of us are to go into the woods and make a clearing there, where we can keep our cattle when the Skrælings come out of the forest. We shall take our bull and keep him to the fore."

The Viking settlers then took up positions in an area of land with the woods on one side and a lake on the other. The Skrælings met them there, and the battle commenced. Many Skrælings were killed. At one point Karlsefni saw one of them pick up an ax that a Viking had dropped. After examining it, the Skræling swung it at one of his fellows, who immediately fell dead. Then a particularly tall and handsome Skræling, whom Karlsefni took to be the leader, took the ax and threw it into the waters of the lake. The Skrælings then fled into the forest.

Although victorious, Karlsefni decided that he no longer wished to stay in Vinland, and the following spring the Vikings loaded their ship with the goods they had collected and returned home to Greenland.

Freydis Voyages to Vinland

The Skrælings notwithstanding, Vinland was considered an excellent source of wealth and fame. Shortly after Karlsefni returned to Greenland, another ship arrived from Norway. Its commanders, two brothers named Helgi and Finnbogi, spent the winter there. One day they were visited by Freydis, the daughter of Eirik the Red, who asked if they would be willing to accompany her on a voyage to Vinland, with an equal share of any profits made. They agreed, and her brother Leif Eiriksson told her that she could use his houses while she was there.

Freydis had an agreement with Helgi and Finnbogi whereby each party would take thirty men (in addition to women) on the voyage. However, Freydis secretly broke this agreement and concealed five more men on her ship. The two ships sailed in convoy to Vinland, the brothers' vessel arriving shortly before Freydis's. By the time Freydis arrived, Helgi and Finnbogi had transferred their supplies to Leif's houses.

As her crew unloaded their ship, Freydis asked Helgi and Finnbogi why they had put their cargo in her brother's houses, to which they replied that, surely, it was part of their agreement that the houses should be shared.

Freydis shook her head, saying: "Leif lent the houses to me — not to you."

The brothers regarded each other incredulously, and Helgi replied: "We brothers could never be a match for you in wickedness."

Nevertheless, they moved their belongings out of the houses and built their own, farther inland, on the bank of a nearby lake.

As the winter grew more severe, the brothers suggested that they entertain themselves by holding various games; but trouble broke out between the two groups, and such was the ill feeling that they played no more games, and for the rest of that winter they did not speak to each other.

One morning, Freydis got up very early and went to the brothers' house. Helgi was out, but Finnbogi was lying awake in bed. Seeing her standing in the doorway, he asked her what she wanted.

"I want you to come outside with me," she replied. "I want to talk to you."

Finnbogi did as she asked, and together they walked to a tree trunk beside the house and sat down on it. Freydis asked how the brothers were getting along, and Finnbogi replied that, while he liked the country, he did not like the enmity that had arisen between the two groups, especially since there was no reason for it.

Freydis agreed with him, saying, "I feel the same as you do. But the reason I came to see you is that I would like to exchange ships with you and your brother. You have the bigger ship, and I wish to go away from here."

Finnbogi agreed to the exchange, and with that he went back to his bed, and Freydis returned to her own house. When she climbed into bed, her husband, Thorvard, noticed that she was cold, and asked her where she had been. Freydis then flew into a pretend rage, crying, "I went to see the brothers and offered to buy their ship, but they grew angry and struck me and handled me roughly. But you are a wretch who would never avenge either my humiliation or your own. Unless you avenge me, I shall divorce you!"

Thorvard was stung terribly by these taunts, and of course knew that under Icelandic law his wife had the right to divorce him and claim half of his possessions. Without delay he roused his men and told them to grab their weapons.

They went straight to the brothers' house and burst in on them while they were asleep. Thus unprepared, the brothers and their men were tied up, dragged outside, and killed. The only ones left alive were the five female members of the brothers' group. None of Thorvard's men were willing to kill them, so Freydis took an ax and killed the women herself.

They then returned to their own house, Freydis congratulating herself on the cleverness of her plan. She warned her companions that should they ever return to Greenland, she would have anyone killed who breathed a word about what had happened. "Our story," she said, "will be that the others stayed on here when we left."

And so that spring they loaded the brothers' ship with all the cargo they had accumulated and set sail for Greenland, arriving at Eiriksfjord early in the summer. When they arrived, they found Karlsefni ready to sail to Iceland with the richest load of any Viking ship.

Karlsefni's Line

Freydis returned to her farm, after paying her companions plenty of money to keep them quiet about the dreadful crime that had been committed in far-off Vinland. It is very difficult to keep such horrors secret, however, even when one's tongue has been numbed by wealth. Eventually, rumors of some terrible crime having been committed during the expedition reached the ears of Freydis's brother Leif. He was sickened by what he heard, and took three of her men and tortured them until they revealed every detail of what had happened. They were interrogated separately, and their stories were exactly the same.

"I do not have the heart to punish my sister as she deserves," Leif said. "But I prophesy that her descendants will never prosper."

From that moment on, Freydis and her family were hated and mistrusted by everyone.

Karlsefni sailed to Norway, where he sold his cargo and enjoyed the praise heaped on him and his wife by all whom they met. The following spring he prepared to sail to Iceland. While he was waiting for a favorable wind, a man from Bremen in Saxony came to see him, and asked if he were prepared to sell his ship's ornately carved gablehead.

Karlsefni replied that he did not want to sell it.

The Saxon persisted. "I shall give you half a mark of gold for it," he said.

This was a very good offer, and Karlsefni agreed. The gablehead had almost certainly been carved by Tyrkir, the Saxon who had discovered the wild grapes that had given Vinland its name and who was a skilled craftsman.

Karlsefni then put to sea and arrived at Skagafjord, in northern Iceland. The following spring he bought lands at Glaumby and set up home with his wife, Gudrid, and their son, Snorri, who had been born in Vinland. Karlsefni farmed there for the rest of his life, and was considered a man of great stature by everyone.

After his death, Gudrid and Snorri took over the farm; and when Snorri married, Gudrid went on her pilgrimage to Rome. Upon her return to Glaumby, she found that Snorri had built a church there. She became a nun, and remained there for the rest of her life, thus fulfilling the prophecy of her first husband, Thorstein Eiriksson.

Snorri had a son called Thorgeir, who had a daughter named Yngvild. Her son became Bishop Brand Sæmundarson, bishop of Holar in northern Iceland. Snorri also had a daughter named Hallfrid, who married Runolf and had a son who became Bishop Thorlak Runolfsson, bishop of Skalholt in southern Iceland.

Fact and Fantasy

The Viking attempt to colonize North America lasted just three years, and ultimately failed because of the increasing hostility of the natives, who vastly outnumbered the Norse settlers. Although initial relations were, as we have seen, reasonably cordial, the Native Americans inevitably came to realize that the newcomers were exploiting them. Their furs and pelts were very valuable, and they were being asked to trade them for goods of far less worth. According to *Grænlendinga Saga*, the Vikings offered them milk; while *Eirik's Saga* mentions red cloth, which they offered in smaller and smaller strips as their supplies diminished. In the end, as Magnus Magnusson succinctly puts it in *The Vikings*, "Europe . . . was not yet ready to colonise America."

He continues:

Did it leave any mark, this abortive attempt to bring North America into the ambit of North Europe? Yes, indirectly — in the form of a welter of wishful thinking. Canadians would like to claim Vinland as theirs because of the saga references to maple trees and maple wood; the maple leaf is now the national emblem of Canada, and *Grænlendinga Saga* says that when Thorfinn Karlsefni visited Norway after his Vinland adventure, one of the souvenirs he traded was a carved gable-head of maple wood. Americans, on the other hand, would also like to claim Vinland as theirs because they find it hard to resist the temptation to push back the frontiers of their cultural heritage as far as possible beyond the relatively recent sixteenth century to the more distant Viking Age.

This has led to some quite bizarre claims for a Viking presence much farther south and inland, including a seventeenth-century windmill at Newport, Rhode Island. The most ridiculous "relic" presented so far is the artifact known as the Kensington Stone, which first came to public attention in 1898. The story goes that it had been discovered embedded in the roots of a poplar tree near the village of Kensington in Minnesota. It was allegedly found by a Swedish immigrant named Olof Ohman. The dark gray slab was about 30 inches high, 16 inches wide, and 5 inches thick.

Although the long inscription on the face of the slab bore some resemblance to medieval runic lettering, it was later identified as a mixture of modern Swedish, Norwegian, Danish, and English. Magnusson offers us a rough English translation:

8 Goths [Swedes] and 22 Northmen on a journey of exploration westward from Vinland. Our camp was by two skerries one day's journey north from this stone. We were out fishing one day. When we came home, found 10 men red with blood and dead. AVM [Ave Maria?] save us from evil. Have ten men by the sea to look after our ships, 14 days' journey from this island. 1362.

Scandinavian scholars lost no time in dismissing the Kensington Stone as an obvious forgery. In 1907 it was acquired by a man named Hjalmar Rued Holand, a Wisconsin impresario who relentlessly argued the case for the stone's authenticity for the next fifty years. His persistence eventually paid off somewhat, and Holand managed to persuade several distinguished authorities to take the Kensington Stone seriously. In 1948, the stone received what was perhaps the ultimate endorsement when it was put on display at the Smithsonian Institution in Washington.

However, this respectability was not to last. The great runic scholar Professor Sven B. F. Jansson examined the stone and reported that it was indeed a forgery. Ten years later, another scholar, Erik Wahlgren, proved once and for all that the Kensington Stone was not what Holand had claimed it to be. Wahlgren's investigations, detailed in his 1958 book *The Kensington Stone: A Mystery Solved*, revealed that the stone's alleged discoverer, Olof Ohman, was not the simple, uneducated farmer described by Holand. He was actually an intelligent, self-educated man with a keen interest in mysticism. He owned many books, including Carl Rosander's *The Well-Informed Schoolmaster*, a popular encyclopedia originally published in Sweden in 1864, and reprinted a number of times in both Sweden and the United States. This book contained a good deal of information on the history of the Swedish language, beginning with the runes.

According to Magnusson:

> We can now understand the *how* and the *why* of this classic American hoax. America was in a fever of excitement over the Chicago World['s] Fair of 1893 ("The [World's] Columbian Exposition"), which had featured so dramatically Magnus Andersen's epic sailing of a near-replica of the Gokstad Ship from Norway to North America. . . . The atmosphere was right for forgery, Scandinavian immigrants in America were in the right mood to accept one, and the whole world was geared to thinking about Vikings in North America.

Probably the most famous forgery of Viking artifacts is the so-called Vinland Map, an allegedly fifteenth-century chart of the Atlantic that included the Vinland of the Norse sagas. Measuring approximately 11 by 16 inches, it is a pen-and-ink drawing of the world. On the reverse side there is an inscription, "Delineation of the first, second, and third parts of the *Speculum*." The astonishing thing about the map is that it includes the Viking Atlantic settlements in its northwestern corner, including a large island labeled *Vinilanda Insula*. In the top left-hand corner there is a Latin inscription that begins:

By God's will, after a long voyage from the island of Greenland to the south toward the most distant remaining parts of the western ocean sea, sailing southward amid the ice, the companions Bjarni and Leif Eiriksson discovered a new land, extremely fertile and even having vines, the which island they named Vinland.

The map was published by Yale University Press in 1965 in a book entitled *The Vinland Map and the Tartar Relation*. *The Tartar Relation* was a previously unknown twenty-one-page account of the Franciscan Friar John de Plano's mission to the Mongol court from 1245 to 1247. According to the volume's editors, the map must have been made in about 1440, and was based on a map of the world drawn by the Venetian cartographer Andrea Bianco in 1436, combined with a chart probably made by a Norse cartographer in the thirteenth century.

The history of the map is a complex one, and was given in an account by Dr. Helen Wallis, superintendent of the map room of the British Library in 1974. In 1957 Enzo Ferrajoli, an Italian bookseller living in Barcelona, showed the map to various other booksellers in Geneva, London, and Paris on behalf of an unnamed client. Included with the map was a previously unknown account of a mission to the Mongol court by a Franciscan friar named John de Plano Carpini.

At this point a London bookseller named Joseph Irving Davis, of Davis and Orioli Ltd., helped Ferrajoli have the map inspected at the British Library. The scholars at the British Library were reluctant to accept the authenticity of the document, noting that the wormholes on the Map and *The Tartar Relation* did not match, and that the Latin of the inscriptions was suspect. Their conclusion was that the map was not genuine.

Ferrajoli took the document back to Geneva and sold it for $3,500 to Laurence Witten, an antiquarian bookseller from New Haven, Connecticut. He took it to Yale University and had it examined by two scholars who, like their British colleagues, were not convinced that the map was genuine. His doubts notwithstanding, one of the scholars, Alexander O. Vietor, curator of maps at the Yale University Library, asked for a "first refusal" option on *The Tartar Relation*. In an interview with Magnus Magnusson on the BBC-TV program *Chronicle* in 1966, Vietor stated that they were intrigued by the book, in spite of its relatively modern binding, and the fact that the wormholes on the surface of the map did not coincide with the single wormhole on the front page of *The Tartar Relation*, which implied that the two documents did not belong together.

Magnusson writes:

But now the long arm of coincidence — too long, some might think — stretched out, right on cue to allay Vietor's doubts. It just so happened that the London bookseller, Joseph Davis, had bought from Enzo Ferrajoli, the Italian bookseller, another work reputedly from that same private library which had provided the Map and *The Tartar Relation*. This was a "rather sorry" fragment of a fifteenth-century copy of a thirteenth-century work called the *Speculum Historiale* (*Mirror of History*) by Vincent de Beauvais. It was advertised at a price of £75 in the 1958 Davis and Orioli catalogue, where it was spotted and purchased by Thomas Marston as a routine acquisition for the Yale University Library. He happened to show it to Laurence Witten — and now what has been sardonically called "a miraculous re-union" occurred.

Alexander Vietor stated that Witten noticed how the wormholes on the Vinland map coincided exactly with those on the *Speculum Historiale*. He then examined the back of the *Speculum Historiale* and discovered that its single worm-hole exactly matched the single wormhole on the front of *The Tartar Relation*. This incredible coincidence seemed to establish that *The Tartar Relation*, the *Speculum Historiale*, and the Vinland map itself had all once been bound together, thus strongly implying a fifteenth-century date for the map. As Magnusson wryly comments, these three documents had all come from the same private library, had somehow been separated, and then had come on the market "in a manner which can only be described as providential" at precisely the right moment to establish the authenticity of the Vinland map.

The three documents were bought by an anonymous Yale benefactor (possibly Paul Mellon) for £100,000, who do-nated them to the Yale University Library. The task of edit-ing them for publication took seven years. The results were condemned by many scholars, most notably the highly re-spected English cartographist Professor Eva Taylor, who pointed out that Greenland was drawn as an island on the map — a fact that was only established by explorers in the late nineteenth century. She added that the degree of accu-racy with which Greenland had been rendered strongly im-plied that it had simply been traced from a modern atlas.

Further refutation of the claims for the Vinland map's au-thenticity came in 1967, when it was exhibited at the British Museum. Scientists from the museum's research laboratory examined the map under ultraviolet light and found that the ink did not match that of the other documents. When they informed Yale University of their findings, it began its own investigation. Yale contracted the analysis to a Chicago firm of specialists in small-particle analysis, and in 1972 they presented their findings. It was the final nail in the coffin of the Vinland map. The report stated that the inks used in *The Tartar Relation* and the *Speculum Historiale* were definitely medieval and contained organic iron gallotannate. The ink on the Vinland map, however, contained an inorganic substance called titanium dioxide, which was not developed until 1917. The Vinland map was, after all, a twentieth-century forgery.

5

New Lives in the East

*I have seen the Rús as they come on their merchant jour-
neys, and stay encamped on the Volga. I have never seen
more perfect specimens, tall as date palms, blond and
ruddy. Each man has an ax, a sword and a knife which
he keeps by him at all times. Each woman wears neck
rings of gold, one for each thousand dinars her master
owns.*

— Ibn Fadlan

Along the Rivers of Russia

While the Norwegians concentrated on their expansion west
across the Atlantic Ocean to Iceland, Greenland, and ultimately (if only temporarily) Vinland, Swedish traders were
sailing far up Russia's rivers to take advantage of the lucrative
trade routes of the East. These Scandinavians were known as
Rús and Væringjar, or Varangian. Rús probably is derived
from *Ruotsi*, the Finnish word for the Swedes, which is in
turn derived from the Scandinavian *róðr*, meaning a ship's
crew. Russia derives its name from the Rús, and this term
refers to only those Scandinavians living in Russia. The word
"Varangian" is derived from the Old Norse *várar*, meaning

pledge or oath. This word dates from about the mid-tenth century and was used to distinguish newly arrived Scandinavians from the Slavicized Rús.

The Scandinavian expansion east of the Baltic began early, in about 650, although it was motivated primarily by trade. By the end of the eighth century, Arab merchants had begun to penetrate the Volga, introducing high-quality silver coinage into the area. Understandably intrigued, the Rús began to move farther inland in an attempt to identify the source. By the middle of the ninth century they had completed their exploration of the Russian river system, and had established trade contacts with both the Arab traders on the Volga and the Byzantines at Constantinople.

Life was not all peaceful trade, however: Russia was a dangerous place, and the routes through it could hide many perils, including local Slavs and steppe nomads, who frequently attacked trade convoys. One of the most dangerous places was the area around the Dnieper River rapids south of Kiev. These rapids were impassable by boats, which had to be drawn overland. The Vikings themselves frequently used the trade routes to launch raids on Constantinople and the surrounding areas, although they were not particularly successful.

By the second half of the ninth century, the Rús had established a state based at Kiev and Novgorod. The primary documentary source for this period is known as the *Russian Primary Chronicle*, which was originally compiled early in the twelfth century in Cave Monastery outside Kiev. According to the *Chronicle*, the "Varangians from beyond the sea" imposed a tribute on the local Slav tribes but were expelled by them:

[A.D. 860–862] The tributaries of the Varangians drove them back beyond the sea and, refusing them further tribute, set out to govern themselves. But there was no law among them, and tribe rose against tribe. There arose strife among them and they began to fight among themselves. And they said to themselves: "Let us find a king to rule over us and make judgments according to the law." And they crossed the sea to the Varangians, to the Rús; for these Varangians were called Rús as others were called Swedes, others again Norwegians or Angles or Goths. And to the Rús [they] said: "Our land is large and rich, but there is no order in it. So come and be king and rule over us."

And three brothers with their kinsfolk were chosen; they brought with them all the Rús and came here. The eldest, Rurik, settled in Novgorod; the second, Sineus, settled in Beloozero; and the third, Truvor, settled in Izborsk.

And from these Varangians the Russian land got its name, especially the district of Novgorod. The present inhabitants of Novgorod are descended from the Varangian race, but earlier they were Slavs.

After two years, Sineus and his brother Truvor died, and Rurik assumed sole authority. He distributed the towns to his men — Polotsk to one, Rostov to another, Beloozero to a third.

Like the Icelandic sagas, this account was written long after the events it describes and thus should be treated with caution. In *The Vikings,* Magnus Magnusson offers a slightly different account in another version of the *Chronicle* known as the *Codex Hypatianus:*

They took with them all the Rús and came first to the Slavs, and they built the city of Ladoga [modern Staraya Ladoga]. Rurik, the eldest, settled in Ladoga; Sineus, the second, settled at Beloozero; and Truvor, the third, settled at Izborsk. From these Varangians the land of Rús received its name. After two years Sineus died, as well as his brother Truvor, and Rurik assumed sole authority. He than came to Lake Ilmen and founded on the River Volkhov a city they named Novgorod.

The *Russian Primary Chronicle* states that in 880, Rurik's successor Oleg captured the hilltop town of Kiev, declaring that it should be the mother of Russian cities. To consolidate his position he began to build stockaded towns, and then imposed tribute on the neighboring tribes, probably in the form of furs, cash, and slaves.

In about the year 920, an Arab geographer named Ibn Rustah wrote an account of how the Rús lived during this period. He described how they fought regularly with the Slavs, using ships to attack them, and sold their captives as slaves. They had no villages or estates: their only occupation was trade in various animal skins, including sable and squirrel. They took coins as payment, which they fastened into their belts.

> They have many towns. They are generous with their possessions, treat guests honorably, and act handsomely toward strangers who take refuge with them, and all those who accept their hospitality. . . .
>
> When a leading man among them dies, they dig a grave like a big house and put him inside it. With him they put his clothes and the gold armrings he wore and also much food and drinking vessels and coins. They also put his favorite wife in the grave with him while she is still living; then the entrance to the grave is stopped up, and she dies there.

Over the years there has been considerable debate as to the exact nature of the Scandinavian contribution to the creation of Russia. Western scholars maintained that until the arrival of the Vikings, Russia was a dark and undeveloped land, and it was Swedish explorers who saw its vast potential as an area of trade with both Scandinavia and the Far East. Russian scholars disagree with this hypothesis, and maintain that the role of the Vikings in the development of the Russian state was quite small. In an interview with Magnus Magnusson, the distinguished Russian academician B. A. Rybakov stated that the Russian state had already existed for three hundred years before the arrival of the Vikings. A nucleus of tribes existed around the middle Dnieper in the sixth century and later formed the Kiev state. Rybakov added that the nucleus of tribes expanded, "and it may well be that Vikings were attracted here by the glamour of the Kiev state, and because the Kiev state traded actively with Constantinople."

The Slavic peoples of eastern Europe had achieved a level of social and technological development very similar to that of the Vikings, with considerable skills in ironworking and farming. The only qualities the Vikings brought with them that the Slavs did not already possess were unity and leadership. According to the historian John Haywood, "the limited nature of Scandinavian cultural influence on the development of early Russia is immediately obvious from the fact that there are only six or seven Scandinavian loan words in the Russian language."

Of far greater importance to the cultural development of Kievan Russia was the influence of Byzantium, which began in earnest with the conversion to Orthodox Christianity of the Russian prince Vladimir (978–1015) in 989. Eighty-two years earlier, in 907, Rurik's successor Oleg had taken a huge fleet down the Dnieper River and into the Black Sea, with his sights set on Constantinople. The city's defenders moored heavy iron chains across the Bosporus in an attempt to stop the advance; but the hardy Rús simply followed their usual habit of portage (i.e., pulling their ships out of the water, placing them on rollers, and pulling them over the land). In this manner they were able to bypass the obstacles in the water altogether.

With an army of fearsome Rús at his gates, the emperor had little choice but to sign a treaty giving Russian merchants a wide range of generous terms, including low customs duties, entry visas, access to markets, and even an unlimited number of free baths.

To the Vikings, Constantinople contained wonders and splendors unheard of in their starkly beautiful but harsh homelands. They called it Mikligarðr (Great City). Even in the tenth century, Constantinople was a vast and teeming metropolis of half a million people, an enchanted city of a myriad of domes and spires forming a bridge between the East and the West, a glittering avenue of trade between the two halves of the world. Although splendid and exotic, the streets of Constantinople could be very dangerous places, attracting tough mercenaries as well as merchants and traders. This did not bother the fearless Norsemen, however, and after so long at the oars of their ships and at dull trading settlements, it is hardly surprising that they took full advantage of the pleasures and perils in Constantinople's bustling streets and alleyways.

Influences of the Byzantine Empire traveled back through Russia to Sweden and Gotland. Many goods and fashions found their way to Scandinavia, including colored, glazed clay eggs, symbolizing the Resurrection and made near Kiev. Tales of the splendors of Constantinople inspired saga writers such as Snorri Sturluson to write of voyages to the city and the wonders witnessed there, as with these lines by the poet Bolverk Arnorsson, quoted by Sturluson in *King Harald's Saga*:

Bleak showers lashed dark prows
Hard along the coastline;
Iron-shielded longships
Flaunted colored rigging.
The great prince saw ahead
The copper roofs of Constantinople;
His swan-breasted ships swept
Toward the tall-towered city.

For a Viking warrior, there could be no greater honor than to be chosen to serve in the Varangian Guard, the emperor's elite bodyguard, which Magnusson describes as a "Brigade of Guards, Royal Marines and Commandos in one." Aside from their duties as bodyguards, they also were used as shock troops in battle, and as imperial policemen charged with the emperor's dirty work, such as arresting patriarchs who had fallen into disfavor.

According to contemporary sources, the Varangian Guard

was composed of mounted infantry; in other words, it was their practice to ride to the theater of battle and then dismount and fight on foot. One such source, written by Asochik of Armenia, describes an argument between Varangians and Iberians that got out of hand in the year 1000:

> A certain soldier from the Russian infantry was carrying hay for his horse, when one of the Iberians went up to him and took the hay away from him. At this another Russian came running up to help his fellow countryman, and the Iberian now called for help from his compatriots.

The fight quickly spread, and by the time it was over some six thousand Varangians had become involved, and thirty Iberians lay dead.

Military units had a slave or paid groom to perform menial chores for them and to look after their baggage, with the elite cavalry units having one servant per man. The servants carried with them tents, cookware, and other support equipment. The Varangian Guard's equipment included a knee-length mail shirt, and a conical helmet with noseguard worn over a mail coif. The weapons they carried were the lethal two-handed Viking ax and the spear. In addition, they carried the scramasax, a knife that served multiple purposes, including cutting food at mealtimes.

A Funeral on the Volga

Not all Vikings who died in the East were brought home for burial. The Arab diplomat Ibn Fadlan, who was secretary of an embassy from the caliph of Baghdad to the ruler of the Bulgars of the Middle Volga, wrote a fascinating account of a Viking chieftain's burial in 922:

> I had heard that at the deaths of their chief personages they did many interesting things, of which the least was

cremation, and I was interested to learn more. At last I was told of the death of one of their outstanding men. They placed him in a grave and put a roof over it for ten days while they cut and sewed garments for him.

If the deceased is a poor man they make a little boat, which they lay him in and burn. If he is rich, they collect his goods and divide them into three parts, one for his family, another to pay for his clothing, and a third for making *nabīd* [probably beer], which they drink until the day when his female slave will kill herself and be burned with her master. They stupefy themselves by drinking this *nabīd* night and day; sometimes one of them dies cup in hand.

At the ceremony Ibn Fadlan witnessed, which was a cremation on a ship, the chieftain's family asked his male and female slaves if any of them wished to die with him. One girl replied that she wished to be sacrificed.

When the day of the cremation arrived, Ibn Fadlan went to the river where the chieftain's ship lay and saw that his men had already drawn the ship up onto the shore, and had put a couch covered with Greek brocade on board. A stout, grim-faced old woman arrived. The Vikings called her the angel of death, and she was in charge of the funeral arrangements, including the killing of the slave girl.

The chieftain's body was carried onto a tent that stood on the deck of the ship, whereupon the other Viking leaders had sexual intercourse with the slave girl, each saying to her: "Tell your lord that I did this out of love for him." The girl was then led to an object resembling a door frame, at which she placed her feet on the men's hands and was lifted up so that she might see over the top.

She was lifted thus three times, and the third time she cried out: "I see my master seated in Paradise . . . he calls to me, so let me get to him." She was then taken to the ship, where she took off the two bracelets she was wearing and gave them to the old woman who was to take her life. As the angel of death took the girl's hand and led her into the tent, the men beat their shields with their staves to drown out her screams. They knew that if the other slave girls heard the sounds of what was happening in the tent, they would never allow themselves to be sacrificed also.

The victim was placed by her master's side; two men held her feet and two her hands, while the angel of death looped a cord around her neck and gave the ends to another two men to pull. Then she took a broad-bladed dagger and plunged it repeatedly between the girl's ribs, while the two men strangled her with the cord. The chieftain's closest relative then came forward with a piece of lighted wood. He walked, naked, backward toward the ship, and set fire to the pile of wood that had been placed beneath the vessel. Presently, the flames rose up and engulfed everything — the ship, the tent, the chieftain, and his slave girl.

One of the Rús was standing at Ibn Fadlan's side. He said something the emissary did not understand, and when he asked the interpreter for a translation, the man said: "He said that you Arabs are stupid."

"Why?" asked Ibn Fadlan.

"Because," replied the interpreter, "you take the people you love and honor most and put them in the ground, where worms and insects eat them. But we burn them in the twinkling of an eye, so that they enter Paradise at that very moment."

Epilogue
The End of the Viking Age

We never kneel in battle
Before the storm of weapons
And crouch behind our shields;
So the noble lady told me.
She told me once to carry
My head always high in battle
Where swords seek to shatter
The skulls of doomed warriors.
— Snorri Sturluson, *King Harald's Saga*

The Norsemen did not go quietly into the night of history; the end of their age went with a bang, not a whimper. For three hundred years they had been the scourge of Europe, their lightning raids and prolonged and troublesome settlement on the Continent leaving an indelible mark on its history and culture. But the Vikings constituted a small force compared to the lands and societies through which they plundered their way, and it was inevitable that Europe's influence on them was far greater than any they themselves could wield. By the year 1200, Scandinavia was completely integrated into Latin Christendom, but this integration was preceded by a final explosion of raiding and conquest.

The Scandinavian kingdoms were not sufficiently developed to raise reliable tax revenues from their subjects. The solution to this problem was quite simple: an income sufficient to run the kingdoms could be raised by continued raiding, especially around the British Isles. Another problem the kingdoms faced was the steady decline in supplies of silver, due to the exhaustion after the mid-tenth century of the silver mines of the Islamic world, which had greatly helped to drive the Scandinavian economy. Ultimately this led to the abandonment of the trade routes in the East, and for the first time the raiding expeditions toward the south and west included Swedish Vikings.

It was a fairly straightforward matter to mount raids on the coastal communities in western England, in Wales, and in Ireland. The Norsemen already possessed settlements in the northern and western isles of Scotland, which served as useful headquarters for predatory expeditions long after the Vikings had curtailed their raiding in other parts.

Eastern England suffered to a much greater extent from these final raids, which began as traditional small pirate expeditions but quickly developed into full-scale plundering and tribute-gathering affairs, thanks to Olaf Tryggvason and Svein Fork-Beard and their large, professional armies. Olaf Tryggvason was an experienced pirate who had been active in the Baltic and who now set his sights on the throne of Norway. Olaf was killed in battle in 1000, but Svein went on to become the most successful Viking leader of the period. This was due mainly to his tactic of avoiding destructive attacks in favor of accepting huge bribes of up to 48,000 pounds of silver. In 1013, Svein set sail from Denmark with a huge fleet, intent on finally taking the prize of England. With him was his eighteen-year-old son, Knut.

Svein moved swiftly through the country, taking Wessex, Mercia, and Northumbria. The English king Aethelred the Unready sent his family to Normandy and then fled there himself. While it is true that Aethelred is remembered as one of the most feeble of English rulers, it is not entirely fair to place all the blame for the renewed Viking attacks at his door. The Viking armies were larger and better organized than before, and their lack of desire to establish settlements made counter-attack virtually impossible. Aethelred had come to the throne of England following the death of his father, King Edgar, in 975, the crown having first gone to Aethelred's half brother Edward. The bitter disputes that followed resulted in the murder of Edward while on a visit to Corfe Castle in Dorset, and the accession of the ten-year-old Aethelred to the throne.

Aethelred's problems with the Vikings began almost as soon as he gained the throne. In 980 the Norse raiders descended on Southampton, the Isle of Thanet, and Cheshire. Once again the raids were carried out by small and highly mobile groups that attacked, plundered, and withdrew before an adequate defense could be mobilized. For the next decade the attacks would be more or less constant, with a few short periods of relative calm in between. The raids were enormously damaging to the local areas involved but did little to undermine English society as a whole.

This changed in 991, with the arrival of an enormous Viking war fleet of ninety-three ships in the Thames estuary. Their intention was to plunder the wealthy southeastern portion of the country. One of their leaders was the Norwegian Olaf Tryggvason, who had cut his teeth as a pirate in the Baltic. Tryggvason and his men were doubtlessly expecting to maintain the upper hand throughout the campaign. Of the Vikings' arrival, *The Anglo-Saxon Chronicle* has this to say:

> 991. In this year came [Olaf] with ninety-three ships to Folkestone, and harried outside, and sailed thence to Sandwich, and thence to Ipswich, overrunning all the countryside, and so on to Maldon.
>
> Ealdorman Byrhtnoth came to meet them with his levies and fought them, but they slew the ealdorman there and had possession of the place of slaughter.

We would have known nothing more about this encounter were it not for the anonymous poet who immortalized the events in a poem titled "The Battle of Maldon," which describes the heroic death of Ealdorman Byrhtnoth. In the second week of August, after the highly successful raid on Ipswich, the Vikings entered the Blackwater estuary and made camp on Northey Island, a little way to the east of the town of Maldon, their next intended target. The island was connected to the flats along the southern edge of the estuary (as it is today) by a tidal causeway about 87 yards long.

Ealdorman Byrhtnoth, the senior ealdorman (king's representative) of Essex, took up a position at the landward end of the causeway. His defense force consisted of local militia and his personal hearth troops. The Vikings watched as the defense force assembled, then shouted their demands for gold and silver tributes across the tidal waters covering the causeway. They would be quite prepared, they said, to leave without engaging in battle, which would be an inconvenience to both sides. All they wanted was danegeld; peace could be bought with a simple payment.

Byrhtnoth listened to these demands with increasing anger. He was far from the prime of youth, having been appointed to the office of ealdorman in about 956; nevertheless, he took his responsibilities for the defense of eastern England very seriously. As Magnus Magnusson notes: "He had been brought up in the old school, in which loyalty to one's leader was the paramount virtue, even at the cost of life itself. He was not a man to back away, whatever the odds."

Presently, the tide began to ebb, and the Viking invaders surged across the causeway. However, so narrow was the ribbon of land (a few feet at its widest) that three of Byrhtnoth's retainers held the landward end with ease, halting the Norse raiding force in its tracks. To break this stalemate, a Viking herald made a sly request, which he must have known would be looked on favorably by the proud ealdorman. He asked that the Vikings be allowed to come across the causeway and meet the defenders in a fair fight on equal terms. Surely a man like Byrhtnoth would not deny such a request for fairness in battle.

This tactic had the desired effect. The ealdorman could not help but be swayed by the honorable request of a group of proud warriors to be allowed to fight like men. He ordered his own soldiers to withdraw sufficiently to allow the Vikings to come ashore. Gallant the act may have been, but it also was suicidal foolishness. The Vikings charged across the causeway and joined in vicious, horrific battle with the defenders, each side well aware that there could be no possibility of surrender.

It was not long before the gallant Byrhtnoth was fatally wounded by a Viking spear. As he lay dying, he ordered his men not to give up, to continue with the battle at all costs for the sake of their lands and people. Many of the English defenders broke ranks and fled in disarray; however, the ealdorman's own retainers, his *comitatus*, remained on the field of battle, determined to avenge the death of their leader. They knew that it was hopeless, that the Vikings outnumbered them, that the price for their loyalty to their ealdorman would be the greatest a man could pay; yet they stood their ground and paid the price.

Magnusson quotes the words of one elderly retainer, Byrhtwold, who had spent much of his life in Byrhtnoth's service and who expressed with beauty and succinctness the final stage of the battle:

Mind must be mightier, heart the fiercer,
Courage the greater, as our strength lessens.
Here lies our lord, cut down in battle.
Hero in the dust. Long will he mourn
Who thinks to dodge this battle-play.
I am an old man now; I shall not go from here.
By the side of my lord I wish to lie,
Lie in the dust with the man I loved.

Magnusson recalls how Marshal Bosquet said of the Charge of the Light Brigade that it was magnificent, but it was not war. It was the same with the Battle of Maldon: Byrhtnoth and his retainers behaved with the utmost valor in the face of insurmountable odds, and gave their lives in the process. The Vikings themselves must have thought them mad: although fine and brave warriors, the Norsemen saw no sense in sacrificing one's life meaninglessly; if a battle were about to be lost, it was far better in their eyes to retreat and survive than to fight hopelessly and die.

The sacrifice of their own lives by Byrhtnoth and his men would at least have held some meaning if the fight against the Vikings had been continued with comparable valor elsewhere; but in a cruel and pathetic irony, their deaths were well and truly in vain. The ealdorman had contemptuously refused to pay danegeld to the Vikings, but King Aethelred did not. On the advice of Sigeric, the archbishop of Canterbury, he signed a peace treaty with Olaf Tryggvason that was designed to prevent further Viking invasions and to protect both English and Scandinavian shipping and trade. In addition, 22,000 pounds of gold and silver were to be paid to the Vikings for signing the peace treaty. From then on, Aethelred would be forced to repeat such payments to keep the Vikings from ravaging England. Whether he realized it or not, these ever-increasing amounts of gold and silver served a function that was the very opposite of what he intended and hoped: they were used to pay the wages of Vikings who were enlisted for the next wave of attacks.

The Viking army sailed away with a sizable down payment on the agreed sum. However, they did not leave England, and the following year Aethelred attempted to engage the Viking fleet at sea with his own fleet. Unfortunately, and in keeping with the climate of treachery and betrayal prevailing in England at that time, the ealdorman of East Anglia, Aelfric, informed the Vikings of the king's plans, and they escaped. Aelfric had been one of Aethelred's most trusted retainers, and the king's revenge was concomitantly awful: in 993, he had the ealdorman's son blinded.

Svein Fork-Beard had, in effect, secured England for himself, but he died in February 1014. Following an initial withdrawal back to Denmark, Knut sailed to England with a fleet of two hundred ships in the summer of 1015. The following year he marched on London, where Aethelred had been recalled from Normandy. However, Aethelred died before Knut could reach London, and Knut was acknowledged as king of England. Following a series of engagements with Aethelred's son, Edmund Ironside, the two men decided to partition the kingdom between Edmund, who would take Wessex, and Knut, who would take Mercia and the Danelaw. When Edmund Ironside himself died in November 1016, Knut became king of all England.

Knut reigned for the next twenty years, adopting the ways of Christian kingship, and his generosity to the church in England and Scandinavia resulted in his being the first Scandinavian king to be fully accepted by the other Christian rulers of Europe. In spite of his accomplishments as king, Knut is best remembered as a fool who tried to command the tide to turn back. However, that is not quite what happened.

As Magnus Magnusson reminds us in *The Vikings:*

The story was first recorded a century after his death by the English chronicler Henry of Huntingdon, in his *Historia Anglorum,* compiled around 1130. He wrote that when Knut was at the height of his political power he gave orders for his throne to be placed on the seashore as the tide came in. The traditional site for this curious episode is Bosham Beach, near Chichester on the south coast of England; perhaps it is because Bosham village stands on a little peninsula between two tidal creeks, where the tide comes in very fast, and also has a fine Saxon church which claims to house the mortal remains of one of Knut's young daughters.

So there you have Knut sitting on his throne at the water's edge, surrounded by a gaggle of puzzled courtiers. And he said to the rising tide, according to Henry of Huntingdon, "You are within my jurisdiction, and the land on which I sit is mine; no one has ever resisted my command with impunity. I therefore command you not to rise over my land, and not to presume to wet the clothes or limbs of your lord." But the sea rose as usual, and wetted the king's feet and legs without respect.

This is about as much of the story as most people know, getting the impression that Knut the Great had grown too big for his boots, which got a good soaking as a consequence. But in Henry of Huntingdon's version it does not end there. That is only the first half. And the second half of the story makes it quite clear that the king intended the tide to give him a wetting, as an object lesson in humility for the benefit of the assembled courtiers. It goes on:

> And so the king jumped back on to dry land, and said, "Be it known to all inhabitants of the world that the power of kings is empty and superficial, and that no one is worthy of the name of king except for Him whose will is obeyed by Heaven, earth and sea in accordance with eternal laws."
>
> And with that he took off his golden crown and never put it on his head again.

With Knut's death in 1035 the Anglo-Scandinavian empire he had created began to fall apart, and by 1042 the native royal dynasty returned to power in England in the person of Aethelred's son Edward the Confessor. Following this breakup, Sweden regained full independence, while Denmark was briefly ruled by Norway until the accession of Svein Estrithson in 1046. The new Norwegian king, Harald Hardradi, challenged his claim, and nearly two decades of war followed until Harald accepted Svein's claim to the Danish throne.

Although Denmark, Norway, and Sweden had by this time become reasonably stable kingdoms, each lacked the resources to dominate the others, and each suffered civil wars resulting from elective disputes and other internal quarrels. Christianity played a vitally important part in the consolidation of these kingdoms, thanks to the efforts of Harald Blue-Tooth in Denmark, Olaf Tryggvason in Norway, and Olof Skötkonung in Sweden. The concept of heredity and divinely ordained kingship eliminated the succession disputes that arose from the earlier elective principle. In addition, conversion to Christianity opened the way to easier relations with the rest of western Europe. This brought numerous benefits to Scandinavia, not least of which were the bishoprics whose foundation paved the way for effective centers of administration, which in turn ensured the reliable collection of taxes. Effectively run revenue collection reduced the king's need to finance the running of his kingdom by means of predatory raids overseas. For those Scandinavians who wished to acquire fame, respect, and wealth, the growth of royal government also offered the chance to climb society's ladder through service to the crown, rather than by plundering the lands of others.

For its own part, the church found it advisable to allow the kings a certain level of independence from papal authority; after all, the task of conversion was made easier by a strong monarchy. The boundaries of the bishoprics helped to define the borders of the kingdoms of Scandinavia. "For example," writes the historian John Haywood, "the archbishopric of Uppsala founded in 1164 included the bishoprics of both Svealand and Götaland as well as the bishopric of Åbo in Finland, prefiguring by some years the boundaries of the medieval Swedish kingdom."

In spite of the advantages offered by Christianization, the process was not complete until the late twelfth century, and paganism was still practiced, especially in Sweden, and most notoriously at the cult center at Uppsala. In his *Gesta Hammaburgensis* (c. 1075), the German cleric Adam of Bremen gave an account of a great temple said to stand at Uppsala, and of the strange and hideous rites allegedly practiced there:

In this temple, entirely decked out in gold, the people worship the statues of three gods in such wise that the mightiest of them, Thor, occupies a throne in the middle of the chamber; Woden [Odin] and Fricco [Frey] have places on either side. The significance of these gods is as follows: Thor, they say, presides over the air, and governs the thunder and lightning, the winds and rains, fair weather and crops. The other, Woden — that is, the Furious — carries on war and imparts to man strength against his enemies. The third is Fricco, who bestows peace and pleasure upon mortals. His likeness, too, they fashion with an immense phallus. But Woden they chisel armed, as our people are wont to represent Mars. Thor with his [hammer] apparently resembles Jove. . . .

It is customary . . . to solemnize in Uppsala, at nine-year intervals, a general feast of all the provinces of Sweden. No one is exempted from attendance at this festival. Kings and people, all and singly, send their gifts to Uppsala and, what is more distressing than any kind of punishment, those who have already adopted Christianity redeem themselves through these ceremonies. The sacrifice is of this nature: of every living thing that is male, they offer nine heads, with the blood of which it is customary to placate gods of this sort. The bodies they hang in the sacred grove that adjoins the temple. Now this grove is so sacred in the eyes of the heathen that each and every tree in it is believed divine because of the death or putrefaction of the victims. Even dogs and horses hang there with men, and a Christian told me that he had seen seventy-two bodies suspended promiscuously. Furthermore the songs customarily chanted in the ritual of a sacrifice of this kind are manifold and unseemly; therefore, it is better to keep silence about them.

As with many beliefs and legends concerning the people of the Middle Ages, we must take Adam of Bremen's evocative description with a large grain of salt. As Magnusson reminds us, the Vikings worshiped their gods in the open air, and without the sinister fanaticism implied in Adam's account. At no time did they worship their gods in such elaborately constructed and decorated buildings. However, as Magnusson goes on to remind us, three extremely thick postholes were discovered in the site of the bell tower of the twelfth-century church at Uppsala, which implies the earlier presence of some kind of structure perhaps designed to protect the images of gods that the Vikings undoubtedly worshiped.

Paganism also survived in the form of the West Slavs, or Wends, who were skilled pirates and who attacked Denmark on many occasions. This resulted in an all-out effort by the Danes and the Swedes to conquer and convert Europe's last remaining pagans.

The eleventh century saw the gradual centralization of government throughout the Viking world, including Scotland and the Isles, where the process began in the earldom of Orkney during the reign of Earl Thorfinn the Mighty (1014–1064). Thorfinn was a fine, courageous leader, and saw off a Scottish attempt to recover Caithness in 1035, and conquered Ross, Shetland, and the Isle of Man. The first earl of Orkney to be brought up as a Christian, Thorfinn was a wise ruler: not only did he acknowledge the authority of the Norwegian crown (in spite of his own considerable prestige), he also attempted to establish a coherent and unifying administrative and ecclesiastical structure within his own lands.

When Thorfinn died, his earldom lost control of the Isles. In 1079, Godred Crovan united the Hebrides and the Isle of Man in a kingdom he divided into five regions, and which he ruled until his death in 1095. The independence of the kingdom of the Isles did not last. Following the murder in Lewis of one of his envoys, King Magnus Barelegs of Norway descended on the kingdom, brutally imposing his own authority on it. His raids extended as far as Dublin, which he captured in 1098. Following Godred's death in Ireland in 1104, his son Olaf took over the kingdom, although he recognized Norwegian authority.

In Scotland, the Viking Age continued into the late twelfth century, finally ending with the assimilation of the Norse settlers in the Hebrides into the native Celtic population. The defeat of Godred II of Man by Somerled in a sea battle fought by moonlight led to a heavy and continuing Gaelic influence on the Isles, although Somerled and his successors preferred to continue to acknowledge the authority of Norwegian rather than Scottish kings.

The end of the Viking Age in Scotland saw the rise of a last freewheeling Viking, the Orkney Islander Sven Asleifarson. With the band of eighty followers he maintained at his hall on the island of Gairsay, he raided twice a year. According to the *Orkneyinga Saga,* Asleifarson made his "spring trip" after he had seen to the sowing of seeds on his farm; the trip lasted until the middle of the summer. He then returned home and devoted himself to harvesting his crops and other domestic duties before embarking on his "autumn trip," during which he would conduct raids until the middle of the winter. Asleifarson made a considerable nuisance of himself, descending on communities in the Hebrides, Wales, and Ireland, plundering without mercy. He also indulged in marine piracy, attacking English merchant ships in the Irish Sea. He continued in this way for thirty years, until finally he was killed during a raid on Dublin in 1171.

The activities of Svein Asleifarson constituted a relatively minor inconsistency in the continual lessening of Scandinavian dominion in the thirteenth century. By 1202 the Scots had successfully reclaimed Ross, Caithness, and Sutherland, and intended to do the same with Man and the Isles.

In an attempt to strengthen his authority, the Norwegian king Håkon IV sent his Great Fleet to the Isles in 1263. The Hebrideans were subdued with ease, but the Scots proved more troublesome, and after a defeat at their hands at Largs on the western coast of Scotland, Håkon withdrew to Orkney, where he died soon after. His successor, Magnus VI, ceded Man and the Hebrides to Scotland in 1266, leaving only Orkney and Shetland in Scandinavian hands until Denmark ceded them in the fifteenth century.

It is one of history's ironies that the medieval Christian monarchies into which the Scandinavian lands were transformed themselves became the victims of raids by less settled peoples to the east. The Viking Age effectively ended with the defeat and death of Harald Hardradi of Norway at the Battle of Stamford Bridge in England in 1066, and the failure of the Danish expeditions to England in the wake of the Norman Conquest of the same year.

Nevertheless, some raids continued to be mounted, especially in the Baltic, which King Harald III of Denmark allowed to go unchecked in return for a share of the plunder; and as late as 1153, King Harald Eystein of Norway led a raid on England. At this time, Denmark in particular was having serious problems with raids conducted by the Wendish tribes of pagan Slavs, which continued in spite of retributive Danish raids to the east.

In the thirteenth century, the Danes and the Swedes joined forces in crusades against the Wends, and under King Valdemar II (1202–1241) the Danes enjoyed considerable power and influence in the Baltic before being superseded by the Germans. The Swedes brought the Finnish peoples under control in the mid-eleventh century, and fewer than fifty years later, found the limits of their expansion when they came up against the principality of Novgorod.

This expansion on the European mainland was not shared by Norway, whose geographical location had always forced it to look more to the west than to the east, and thus it had to contend itself with hegemony over the Norse settlements on Iceland and Greenland.

The Viking Age had been characterized by an incredible energy and thirst for wealth, power, and knowledge of the mysteries lying beyond the horizon. They left their mark in blood on the face of Europe, but their deeds have lost none of their power to fascinate as well as appall. The nature of the Vikings is perhaps best summed up in lines quoted by Snorri Sturluson, and attributed to Harald Hardradi shortly before his death at Stamford Bridge in 1066:

> We do not creep in battle under the shelter of shields,
> before the crash of weapons;
> this is what the loyal goddess
> of the hawk's land commanded us.
> The bearer of the necklace told me long ago
> to hold my head high in the din of weapons,
> when the Valkyrie's sword
> met the skulls of men.

Viking Timeline

793   Viking raiders sack the Anglo-Celtic monastery on Lindisfarne.

c. 795   Viking raids on Ireland begin.

c. 800-810 Reign of King Godfrid of Denmark.

810   Death of Charlemagne.

c. 810–827 Reign of King Harald Klak of Denmark.

c. 827–853 Reign of King Horik Godfredsson of Denmark.

c. 840–870 Reign of King Halfdan the Black of Norway.

844–845   Norse raids on Moorish Spain begin. Lisbon and Seville sacked. Al-Ghazal's diplomatic mission to Horik or Turgeis.

c. 851   First Norse raid on Wales.

c. 852   Swedish Rús begin to dominate the Volga region.

c. 853–873 Reign of King Rorik of Denmark.

c. 860   Norse discovery of Iceland. The Rús found Novgorod and Kiev.

870   Vikings begin to settle Iceland.

c. 873–891 Kings Sigfred and Halfdan rule Denmark together.

878	Alfred the Great defeats Guthrum and forces Vikings wishing to settle in England to convert to Christianity. Norway and Orkney Islands unified.
c. 890s	Reign of King Helgi of Denmark, followed by rule of Denmark by King Olaf the Swede.
912	Gongu-Hrolf takes lands in Normandy as vassal of King Charles III; the descendants of the Viking settlers become the Normans.
c. 922	The Arab ambassador Ibn-Fadlan visits the Scandinavian Rús and writes an account of their customs, including their burial rites.
930	First Althing held in Iceland.
c. 935–950	Reign of King Gorm the Old of Denmark.
946	Reign of King Hakon the Good of Norway.
947	Norway adopts Christianity under the reign of King Olaf Tryggvasson.
950–983	Denmark adopts Christianity under the reign of King Harald Blue-Tooth.
982	Eirik the Red discovers Greenland.
983	Start of reign of King Svein Fork-Beard of Denmark.
c. 986	Norse settlement of Greenland.
1000	Iceland converts to Christianity. Death of King Olf Tryggvason.
c. 1000–1005	Leif Eiriksson voyages to Vinland (North America). Attempts to settle there are ultimately prevented by hostility of Skrælings (Native Americans).
1014	Brian Boru defeats the Vikings in Ireland at the Battle of Clontarf.
1066	King Harald Hardradi of Norway is killed at the Battle of Stamford Bridge during an attempted invasion of England. Harold Godwinsson, the victor at Stamford Bridge, is himself killed at the Battle of Hastings by the army of Duke William

	of Normandy. With the defeat at Stamford Bridge and the Norman Conquest, Viking activity in England ends.
c. 1075	Adam of Bremen writes *Gesta Hammaburgensis ecclesiæ pontificum*.
c. 1122	Ari Thorgilsson (Ari the Learned) writes *Íslendingabók*.
c. 1185– 1223	Saxo Grammaticus writes *Gesta Danorum*.
c. 1200– 1450	Icelandic sagas are written. *Orkneyinga Saga* written by unknown author.
c. 1220– 1225	Snorri Sturluson writes *The Prose Edda* and *Heimskringla*.
c. 1230	*Egil's Saga* written, probably by Snorri Sturluson.
c. 1245	*Laxdæla Saga* written by unknown author.
c. 1250– 1300	Most of the poems of *The Poetic Edda* are collected and written down in the *Codex Regius*.
c. 1300	*Sturlunga Saga*, a collection of Icelandic sagas, is compiled.

Viking Kings

Denmark

1074–1080 Harald III
1080–1086 Knut the Holy
1086–1095 Olaf Hunger
1095–1103 Eirik the Evergood

Norway

c. 880–930 Harald Fine-Hair
c. 930–
c. 936   Eirik Bloodax (deposed)
c. 936–960 Hakon the Good
c. 960–970 Harald Gray-Cloak
995–1000   Olaf Tryggvason
1015–1030   Olaf Haraldson
1030–1035   Svein Alfivason (deposed)
1035–1046   Magnus the Good
1045–1066   Harald Hardradi
1066–1069   Magnus II
1067–1093   Olaf the Peaceful
1093–1095   Hakon Magnusson
1093–1103   Magnus III Bare Legs

Sweden

c. 829   Bjorn
c. 850   Olaf
980–995   Eirik the Victorious
995–1022   Olof Skötkonung
1022–1050   Anund Jacob
1050–1060   Emund the Old
1060–1066   Stenkil Ragnvaldsson
1066–1070   Halsten (deposed)
1070–?   Hakon the Red
?–1080   Inge I (deposed)
1080–1083   Blot-Sven
1083–1110   Inge I (restored)

Bibliography and Suggested Further Reading

I have found several books of particular value in preparing this book. Magnus Magnusson's *The Vikings* is a vivid and highly readable account of the Norsemen and their history. Else Roesdahl's book of the same name has a great deal of fascinating information on archaeology and Viking culture and society. *The Norse Myths*, a retelling of the tales of Scandinavian mythology by Kevin Crossley-Holland, is a superb introduction to the subject, and was of particular help to me in describing the construction of the walls of Asgard in chapter 2.

Almgren, Bertil, ed. *The Viking*. New York: Crescent Books, 1975.

Arbman, Holger. *The Vikings*. London: Thames and Hudson, 1962.

Binns, Alan. *Viking Voyagers: Then and Now*. London: Heinemann, 1980.

Brent, Peter. *The Viking Saga*. New York: Putnam, 1975.

Brønsted, Johannes. *The Vikings*. London: Penguin Books, 1965.

Clarke, Helen, and Björn Ambrosiani. *Towns in the Viking Age*. New York: St. Martin's Press, 1991.

Cohat, Yves. *The Vikings: Lords of the Seas*. New York: Harry N. Abrams, 1992.

Crossley-Holland, Kevin. *The Norse Myths*. New York: Pantheon Books, 1980.

Foote, Peter, and David M. Wilson. *The Viking Achievement: The Society and Culture of Early Medieval Scandinavia*. New York: St. Martin's Press, 1990.

Graham-Campbell, James, ed. *Cultural Atlas of the Viking World*. New York: Facts On File, 1994.

Haywood, John. *The Penguin Historical Atlas of the Vikings*. London: Penguin Books, 1995.

Hollander, Lee M. (trans.) *Heimskringla*. University of Texas Press, 1964.

Jesch, Judith. *Women in the Viking Age*. Woodbridge, England: Boydell Press, 1991.

Jones, Gwyn. *A History of the Vikings*. Oxford: Oxford University Press, 1968.

Larrington, Carolyne, transl. *The Poetic Edda*. Oxford: Oxford University Press, 1996.

Loyn, H. R. *The Vikings in Britain*. New York: St. Martin's Press, 1977.

Magnusson, Magnus, *The Vikings*. Stroud, Eng.: Tempus Publishing Ltd., 1980.

Magnusson, Magnus, and Hermann Pálsson, trans. *The Vinland Sagas (Grænlendinga Saga and Eirik's Saga)*. London: Penguin Books, 1965.

Marsden, John. *The Fury of the Northmen: Saints, Shrines, and Sea-Raiders in the Viking Age*. New York: St. Martin's Press, 1993.

Morgan, Kenneth O., ed. *The Oxford Illustrated History of Britain*. Oxford: Oxford University Press, 1984.

Pendlesonn, K. R. G. *The Vikings*. New York: Mayflower Books, 1980.

Randsborg, Klavs. *The Viking Age in Denmark*. New York: St. Martin's Press, 1980.

Richards, Julian. *Blood of the Vikings*. London: Hodder and Stoughton, 2001.

———. *Viking Age England*. London: Batsford, 1991.

Roesdahl, Else. *The Vikings*. London: Penguin Books, 1998.

Sawyer, Peter, ed. *The Oxford Illustrated History of the Vikings*. Oxford: Oxford University Press, 1997.

Simpson, Jacqueline. *The Viking World*. New York: St. Martin's Press, 1980.

Sturluson, Snorri. *The Prose Edda*. Translated by Jean I. Young. Berkeley and Los Angeles: University of California Press, 1992.

———. *Edda*. Edited by Anthony Faulkes. London: Everyman, 1987.

———. *King Harald's Saga*. London: Penguin Books, 1966.

Swanton, Michael, ed. and trans. *The Anglo-Saxon Chronicle*. London: J. M. Dent, 1996.

Virgil. *The Aeneid*. London: Penguin Books, 1958.

Wahlgren, Erik. *The Vikings and America*. London: Thames and Hudson, 1986.

Wilson, David M. *The Vikings and Their Origins*. New York: Thames and Hudson, 1989.

Wooding, Jonathan. *The Vikings*. New York: Rizzoli, 1996.

Index